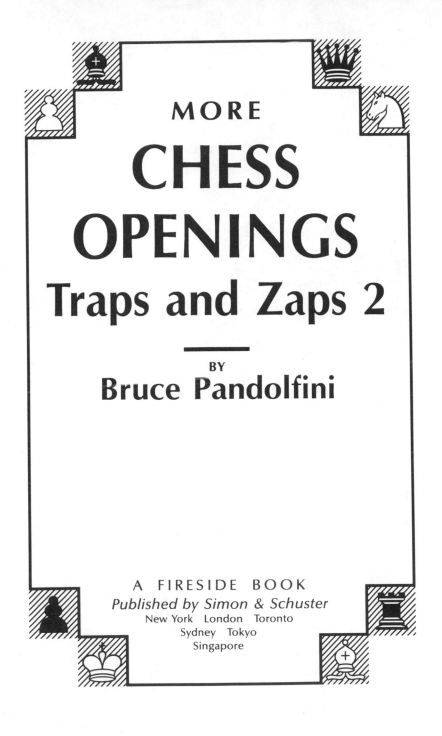

MORE

CHESS
OPENINGS
Traps and Zaps 2

BY

Bruce Pandolfini

A FIRESIDE BOOK
Published by Simon & Schuster
New York   London   Toronto
Sydney   Tokyo
Singapore

FIRESIDE

Rockefeller Center
1230 Avenue of the Americas
New York, New York 10020

Designed by Stanley S. Drate/Folio Graphics Co. Inc.
Manufactured in the United States of America

10 9

Library of Congress Cataloging-in-Publication Data

Pandolfini, Bruce.
    More chess openings : traps and zaps 2 / by Bruce Pandolfini.
        p.   cm.
    "A Fireside book."
    Sequel to: Chess openings / Bruce Pandolfini.
    Includes index.
    1. Chess—Openings.   I. Pandolfini, Bruce.   Chess openings.
    II. Title.
    GV1450.P295   1993   93-20708
    794.1'22—dc20   CIP

ISBN: 0-671-79499-X

Acknowledgments

I would like to thank Bruce Albertson, Carol Ann Caronia, Deirdre Hare, Burt Hochberg, Bonni Leon, David MacEnulty, Idelle Pandolfini, Nick Viorst, and my editor Kara Leverte for putting this book together and making it much better.

For Steve Zaillian and Scott Rudin,
my two favorite filmmakers

Contents

Introduction

Short chess games are powerful lessons. The loser violates a principle. The winner exploits the mistake. It could happen to anyone. Weaken your pawns, they're taken. Attack wildly, your pieces are picked off. Misuse your queen, it's trapped. Neglect development, you're mated. These are lessons the loser never forgets.

More Chess Openings: Traps and Zaps 2 contains 433 short, indelible chess lessons—217 traps and 216 zaps. Like its predecessor, *Chess Openings: Traps and Zaps,* it presents everyday mistakes and their immediate refutations. But unlike its companion volume, *Traps and Zaps 2* features asymmetrical king pawn openings: White begins by moving the king pawn two squares and Black does not. In the earlier collection, each side advanced the king pawn two squares.

In most double king pawn openings, White tries to convert initiative into advantage, and Black tries to hold. But in asymetrical king pawn openings, Black fights for the initiative trom the outset. These openings are generally known as defenses because Black stamps the position, not White.

There are seven main defenses in *Traps and Zaps 2*, presented in six chapters. For each opening, a chart organizes the examples into subgroups and introduces the respective chapter. The Alekhine Defense (1. e4 Nf6), Center Counter Defense (1. e4 d5), Caro-Kann Defense (1. e4 c6), and French Defense (1. e4 e6) all work against the square e4. The Sicilian Defense (1. e4 c5) assaults d4. The Modern and Pirc Defenses attack d4 also, though not in the first few moves. In all these asymetrical systems, Black attempts to usurp the center, throwing caution to the winds.

Traps and Zaps 2 presents 217 main traps, one per page. Each setup position is presented in chart form and shown in a diagram. Study the diagram until you get the winning move. Check the **SOLUTION.** It's explained under **COMMENT.**

Many positions are reinforced by **RELATED ZAPs.** These are short games that echo the main example. Drawn from all openings, there are 216 of them, bringing the total number of games to 433!

For your benefit, the winning tactic of each main example is given at the top of the page. Use it as a clue or for instruction in particular themes. For instance, you can play over forks as a group by finding them in the tactical index in the back. And if you don't know what a fork is, look it up in the glossary. And if you're not sure where to start, turn to page one.

Algebraic Notation

The traps and zaps in this book are given in algebraic notation, a system of recording chess moves that is used throughout the world. In the algebraic system each square has a unique name, consisting of a lowercase letter and a number, with the letter always given first. All squares are named from White's point of view, no matter which side moves. The letters represent files (rows of squares going up and down the board); the numbers stand for ranks (rows of squares going across the board). Diagram A shows all the square names.

BLACK

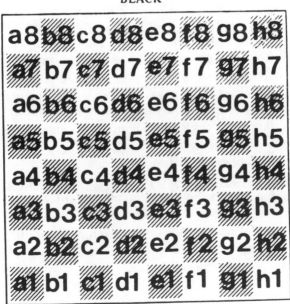

WHITE

Symbols You Should Know

K	King
Q	Queen
R	Rook
B	Bishop
N	Knight

Pawns are not symbolized when recording the moves. But if referred to in discussions, they are named by the letter of the file occupied. Thus, a pawn on the d-file (the file the queens occupy at the start) is a d-pawn. A pawn on d4 is the d-pawn or the d4-pawn.

When a unit moves, symbolize the unit and the square it goes to. If a bishop on f1 moves to c4, write *Bc4*. Note that the piece is capitalized (*B* for bishop) but the square's name is lowercase (*c* for c-file). If the bishop captures something on c4, write *Bxc4* (the *x* means a capture has taken place). The name of the unit captured is not given.

If a pawn makes a capture, merely indicate the file (or square) the capturing pawn starts on and the square it takes on. Thus, if a black pawn on g7 takes any white unit on f6, the move is written *gxf6* or *g7xf6*.

If two similar units can take on the same square, you can distinguish between them by identifying the point of origin. If White has knights on g5 and g3, and the knight on g3 moves to e4, write *N3e4* instead of the plain *Ne4*.

References are often made to specific pieces. A bishop on d7 is the d7-bishop. A rook on a1 is the a1-rook. It may also be useful to distinguish the kingside and the queenside. White's queen knight starts on b1, Black's on b8. Black's king bishop begins on f8, White's on f1. Moreover, bishops travel either on light or dark squares, so each side starts with a light-square bishop and a dark-square bishop.

Other Symbols You Should Know

x	capture
+	check
+ +	mate
0-0	castles kingside
0-0-0	castles queenside
!	good move
?	questionable move
1.	White's first move
1. . . .	Black's first move, if written independently of White's
2.	White's second move
2. . . .	Black's second move, if written independently of White's

Reading the Line Score of a Game

The four moves of the shortest possible chess game are shown in diagrams B-E below and continuing to page 14. The

WHITE'S FIRST MOVE
(DIAGRAM B)
1. f3

BLACK'S FIRST MOVE
(DIAGRAM C)
1. . . . e5

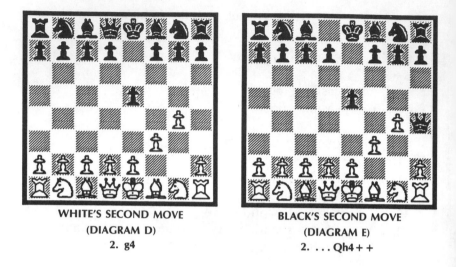

WHITE'S SECOND MOVE
(DIAGRAM D)
2. g4

BLACK'S SECOND MOVE
(DIAGRAM E)
2. ... Qh4 + +

moves are written: **1. f3 e5 2. g4 Qh4 + +**. (This final position is mate).

In this book, the main lines are given in **boldface** type. The analyzed alternatives are given in regular type.

Here's how our little game would look in chart form:

1. f3   e5
2. g4   Qh4 + +

In *More Chess Openings: Traps and Zaps 2,* the setup positions are given in chart form, leaving off at the diagrammed situation. The solutions then follow in line form, which is also the style used for comments and analysis.

MORE
CHESS
OPENINGS
Traps and Zaps 2

SICILIAN DEFENSE

(TRAPS 1-47)
1. e4 c5

TRAPS	WHITE'S 2ND MOVE	BLACK'S 2ND MOVE
1	2. b4	2. . . . cxb4
2	2. c3	2. . . . d6
3	2. Bb5	2. . . . a6
4	2. f4	2. . . . d5
5-6	2. f4	2. . . . Nc6
7-8	2. Nc3	2. . . . d6
9	2. Nc3	2. . . . e6
10-14	2. Nc3	2. . . . Nc6
15	2. d4	2. . . . g6
16-22	2. d4	2. . . . cxd4
23	2. Nf3	2. . . . a6
24-25	2. Nf3	2. . . . g6
26-30	2. Nf3	2. . . . e6
31-38	2. Nf3	2. . . . Nc6
39-47	2. Nf3	2. . . . d6

17

SICILIAN DEFENSE 1

Fork

1. e4	c5
2. b4	cxb4
3. a3	d5
4. exd5	Qxd5
5. axb4?	

BLACK TO MOVE

Solution: White's last move gets back the pawn but loses material. After **5. . . . Qe5 +,** White cannot safeguard his king and threatened rook with one move.

Comment: White begins with a gambit, then violates the spirit of that gambit by spending a move to take back the offered pawn (5. axb4?). Playing 5. Nf3 would leave him down a pawn, but would fuel his initiative and, more important, save a rook.

Related Zap: 1. e4 e4 2. Qh5 g6 3. Qxe5 + (King Pawn Game)

SICILIAN DEFENSE 2

Fork

1. e4	c5
2. c3	d6
3. d4	Nf6
4. dxc5	Nxe4?

WHITE TO MOVE

Solution: White wins a piece with a forking queen check. After **5. Qa4+**, no matter how Black replies, White can continue **6. Qxe4**, garnering the knight.

Comment: In many openings and variations, White guards e4 indirectly with the possibility of a follow-up queen check at a4. Black in turn often has a comparable defense of c5: a queen check at a5.

Related Zap: 1. e4 e5 2. Nf3 d6 3. c3 Nf6 4. d4 Bg4 5. dxe5 Nxe4 6. Qa4+ (Philidor Defense).

Related Zap: 1. e4 e5 2. f4 exf4 3. Be2 d6 4. Nf3 Nf6 5. c3 Nxe4 6. Qa4 (King's Gambit Accepted).

SICILIAN DEFENSE *3*

Trapping

1. e4   c5
2. Bb5   a6
3. Ba4?

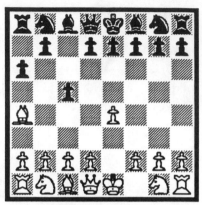

BLACK TO MOVE

Solution: White loses a piece: **3. . . . b5 4. Bb3 c4.**

Comment: White's second move is pointless, allowing Black to attack the bishop with a gain of time. Play mechanically and you'll lose the initiative. Maybe even the game.

Related Zap: 1. e4 e5 2. Nf3 Nc6 3. Bb5 a6 4. Ba4 d6 5. d4 b5 6. Bb3 Nxd4 7. Nxd4 exd4 8. Qxd4 c5 9. Qd5 Be6 10. Qc6 + Bd7 11. Qd5 c4 (Ruy Lopez).

SICILIAN DEFENSE 4

Trapping

1. e4   c5
2. f4   d5
3. Nc3   d4
4. Nd5?

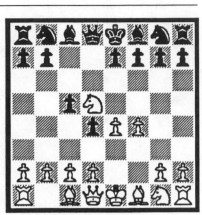

BLACK TO MOVE

Solution: The knight has no place to go after 4. . . . e6.

Comment: Don't cross the frontier line with a knight without a definite purpose. Unless you're prepared to surrender it, make sure it can get back. Once in enemy territory, it's every knight for itself.

Related Zap: 1. d4 f5 2. Nd2 Nc6 3. d5 Nd4 4. e3 (Dutch Defense)

SICILIAN DEFENSE 5

Fork

1. e4	c5
2. f4	Nc6
3. Nf3	d6
4. Bc4	e6
5. e5?	dxe5
6. Nxe5?	

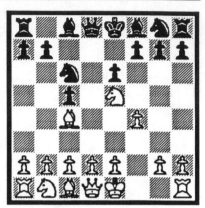

BLACK TO MOVE

Solution: An immediate exchange, **6. . . . Nxe5,** does the trick. After **7. fxe5,** Black forks king and bishop with **7. . . . Qh4 +.**

Comment: White's advance e4-e5 is premature, and White's capturing on e5 with the knight is a blunder. Unless your opponent hands you a golden opportunity, don't begin operations without first preparing. Build your game. Invest in the future.

Related Zap: 1. e4 e5 2. f4 d6 3. Nf3 Nc6 4. Bc4 Be7 5. fxe5 dxe5 6. 0-0 Nf6 7. Nc3 0-0 8. d3 Na5 9. Nxe5 Qd4+ (King's Gambit Declined).

Related Zap: 1. e4 e5 2. Bc4 Bc4 Bc5 3. c3 f6. 4. d4 exd4 5. Qh5 + (Bishop's Opening).

SICILIAN DEFENSE **6**

Fork

1. e4	c5
2. f4	Nc6
3. Nf3	d6
4. Bc4	e6
5. 0-0	g6
6. e5?	dxe5
7. Nxe5?	Nxe5
8. fxe5	

BLACK TO MOVE

Solution: Black steals a piece by **8. ... Qd4+**, forking king and bishop.

Comment: White's offensive is premature. Trying to open lines by advancing the e-pawn, before developing further, backfires. Even after White castles, it's not safe to become aggressive, for White's king is exposed along the open a7-g1 diagonal.

Related Zap: 1. e4 e5 2. f4 exf4 3. Nf3 d5. 4. exd5 Nf6 5. Bb5+ c6 6. dxc6 Nxc6 7. 0-0 Qb6+ (King's Gambit Accepted).

Related Zap: 1. e4 e5 2. Nf3 Nc6 3. Bc4 f6 4. d4 Na5 5. Bxg8 Rxg8 6. dxe5 fxe5 7. Qd5 (Italian Game).

Desperado

1. e4	c5
2. Nc3	d6
3. Nf3	Nc6
4. Bc4	e5
5. d3	Bg4
6. Bxf7 +	Kxf7
7. Ng5 +	

BLACK TO MOVE

Solution: The rude shock **7. . . . Qxg5!** insures that Black stays a piece ahead.

Comment: White assumes that Black must move the king, allowing the g4-bishop to be captured. But since White's queen is hanging, Black can afford to put Black's own queen in jeopardy, exchanging it for the knight. The logic is, take my queen and I'll take yours.

Related Zap: 1. e4 e5 2. Nf3 Nc6 3. Bc4 Bc5 4. Nc3 d6 5. d3 Bg4 6. Bxf7 + Kxf7 7. Ng5 + Qxg5 (Giuoco Piano).

SICILIAN DEFENSE 8
Discovery

1. e4	c5
2. Nc3	d6
3. Nf3	g6
4. d3	Bg7
5. Be2	Nf6
6. 0-0	0-0
7. Bg5	Qa5?
8. Qd2	Rd8?
9. Bh6	Bh8?

WHITE TO MOVE

Solution: Black's queen is helpless after **10. Nd5.** If **10. . . . Qxd2,** then **11. Nxe7** is mate. Nor does 10. . . . Nc6 work, for after 11. Qxa5, Black can't take back without allowing mate.

Comment: Black made three bad moves in a row: a pointless queen move (Qd8-a5); an erroneous rook move (Rf8-d8); and a blunderous bishop move (Bg7-h8). Three strikes and you're out: Nc3-d5!

Related Zap: 1. c4 e5 2. d3 d6 3. Nf3 Nc6 4. g3 Be6 5. Bg2 Qd7 6. 0-0 0-0-0 7. Qa4 Kb8 8. Rd1 Bh3 9. Bh1 Nd4 10. Qxd7 Nxe2++ (English Opening).

SICILIAN DEFENSE 9

Fork

1. e4	c5
2. Nc3	e6
3. Nge2	d5
4. exd5	exd5
5. Nf4	Nf6
6. Bb5+	Nc6
7. d4	Be7
8. dxc5	d4
9. Nce2?	

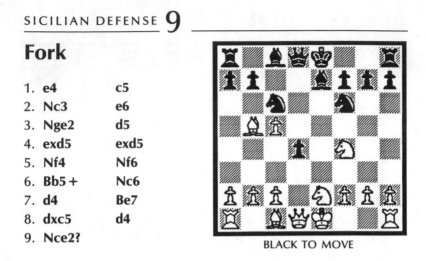

BLACK TO MOVE

Solution: The bishop is dead meat after **9. ... Qa5+**.

Comment: White could still save himself on move nine by taking the c6-knight with check. This stratagem, shifting to offense before responding to an enemy threat, is known as an in-between move, or *zwischenzug*.

Related Zap: 1. e4 e5 2. Nf3 Nc6 3. Nc3 Nf6 4. Bb5 Nd4 5. Nxd4 exd4 6. Ne2 c5 7. d3 Qa5+ (Four Knights Game).

SICILIAN DEFENSE **10**

Trapping

1. e4	c5
2. Nc3	Nc6
3. Nge2	e6
4. g3	d5
5. exd5	exd5
6. Bg2	d4
7. Ne4?	

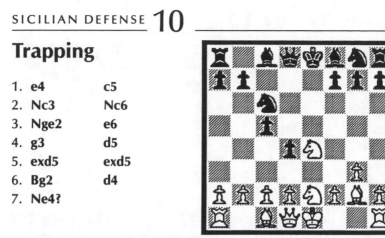

BLACK TO MOVE

Solution: White may have a centralized knight, but it's a dead one after 7. . . . f5.

Comment: Be careful when you make a number of knight moves early in the game, especially when you've held back one or both center pawns. If suddenly attacked by a pawn, an advanced knight could have no place to call home.

Related Zap: 1. c4 e5 2. Nc3 c6 3. g3 d5 4. cxd5 cxd5 5. Bg2 d4 6. Ne4 f5 (English Opening).

SICILIAN DEFENSE **11**

Desperado

1. e4	c5
2. Nc3	Nc6
3. Nge2	Nf6
4. d4	d5
5. exd5	Nxd5
6. dxc5	Ndb4
7. a3	Bf5
8. axb4	Nxb4
9. Ng3	Nxc2 +
10. Qxc2!	Bxc2

WHITE TO MOVE

Solution: White wins the queen back and winds up a piece ahead after **11. Bb5 +**.

Comment: Black leaves himself open for this combination. After 10 moves, no kingside pawns have moved and the only way to get out of check is to block with the queen.

Related Zap: 1. d4 d5 2. c4 e6 3. Nc3 Nf6 4. Bg5 Nbd7 5. cxd5 exd5 6. Nxd5 Nxd5 7. Bxd8 Bb4 + 8. Qd2 Bxd2 + 9. Kxd2 Kxd8 (Queen's Gambit Declined).

SILICIAN DEFENSE 12

Pin

1. e4	c5
2. Nc3	Nc6
3. g3	g6
4. Bg2	Bg7
5. d3	d6
6. Be3	e6
7. Qd2	Qa5
8. Nge2	Nd4
9. Nd1?	

BLACK TO MOVE

Solution: The square c2 may look defended, but White's queen is pinned to its king and can't move. Black wins by 9. . . . Nxc2+ 10. Kf1 Qxd2 11. Bxd2 Nxa1.

Comment: Black often has pressure along the a5-e1 and a1-h8 diagonals, converging on the square c3. To neutralize these attacks, White typically retreats his queen knight to d1 and follows with c2-c3. But this is a problem if c2 is hanging.

Related Zap: 1. c4 e5 2. Nc3 Nc6 3. d3 d6 4. Nf3 Be6 5. Qa4 Qd7 6. Nd5 Nd8 7. Nxc7+ Ke7 8. Qxd7+ Kxd7 9. Nxa8 (English Opening).

SICILIAN DEFENSE 13

Fork

1. e4	c5
2. Nc3	Nc6
3. g3	g6
4. Bg2	Bg7
5. d3	Rb8
6. Be3	Nd4
7. Nce2	Nxe2
8. Nxe2	Bxb2
9. Rb1	Bg7
10. Bxc5	d6
11. Bxa7?	

BLACK TO MOVE

Solution: With **11. . . . Qa5 +**, Black wins the errant bishop.

Comment: The best defenses are often indirect ones. Although Black's a-pawn is not actually guarded on move 11, it might as well be, since the queen can be repositioned for defense with check.

Related Zap: 1. d4 f5 2. e3 e6 3. Bd3 Nf6 4. c4 Bd6 5. Nc3 Ng4 6. c5 Bxh2 7. Rxh2 Nxh2 8. Qh5 + g6 9. Qxh2 (Dutch Defense).

SICILIAN DEFENSE **14**

Skewer

1. e4	c5
2. Nc3	Nc6
3. g3	g6
4. Bg2	Bg7
5. d3	Rb8
6. f4	b5
7. Nf3	b4
8. Ne2	e6
9. a3	Qe7
10. 0-0	bxa3
11. Rxa3	Bxb2?

WHITE TO MOVE

Solution: Black suffers a dark-square deficiency after **12. Bxb2 Rxb2 13. Qa1!** (if 13. . . . Qf6, then 14. e5).

Comment: Black's play is aimless. He neglects kingside development and gives up his flanked bishop to capture an irrelevant pawn. He pays for it diagonally.

Related Zap: 1. Nf3 b6 2. b4 Bb7 3. Bb2 Bxf3 4. gxf3 a5 5. a3 axb4 6. axb4 Rxa1 7. Bxa1 Nf6 8. e3 d6 9. Bb5+ Nbd7 10. f4 Qa8 (Reti Opening).

Fork

1. e4   c5
2. d4   g6
3. dxc5   Na6
4. Bxa6   bxa6?

WHITE TO MOVE

Solution: The winning line is **5. Qd5 Rb8 6. Qe5,** forking the rooks.

Comment: The fianchetto (2. . . . g6) is weakening and out of place. Black should take the d-pawn on move two. Developing the knight to the wing isn't so hot, but it needn't lose a rook. By first playing 4. . . . Qa5 +, Black can take the bishop with the queen.

Related Zap: 1. f4 Nc6 2. b3 e5 3. fxe5 Bc5 4. g3 Bxg1 5. Rxg1 d6 6. exd6 Nf6 7. dxc7 Qd4 (Bird's Opening).

SICILIAN DEFENSE 16

Fork

1. e4   c5
2. d4   cxd4
3. Nf3   e5?
4. Nxe5?

BLACK TO MOVE

Solution: White's capture on e5 is a simple blunder, losing a piece. The forking queen check, **4. ... Qa5 +,** converts the knight to fodder.

Comment: Black's third move is a positional mistake, weakening light squares and the a2-f7 diagonal in particular. After 4. c3 dxc3 5. Nxc3, White would have splendid attacking chances. Instead, White blunders a knight.

Related Zap: 1. e4 e5 2. f4 Bc5 3. Nf3 d6 4. Be2 Nf6 5. c3 Nxe4 6. Qa4 Nc6 7. Qxe4 (King's Gambit Declined).

Unpin

1. e4	c5
2. d4	cxd4
3. Nf3	e5
4. c3	dxc3
5. Nxc3	d6
6. Bc4	Bg4
7. Nxe5!	Bxd1?

WHITE TO MOVE

Solution: White forces mate by **8. Bxf7+ Ke7 9. Nd5++**. Black wins the queen, White the king. Fair is fair.

Comment: The unpinning combination begun with White's seventh move is a version of Legal's sacrifice. It was first recorded in 1750 in a game won by Legal and given below.

Related Zap: 1. e4 e5 2. Nf3 d6 3. Bc4 Bg4 4. Nc3 g6? 5. Nxe5 Bxd1 6. Bxf7+ Ke7 7. Nd5++ (Philidor Defense).

18

Double Threat

1. e4	c5
2. d4	cxd4
3. c3	dxc3
4. Nxc3	e6
5. Nf3	Bb4
6. Qd4	Nc6
7. Qxg7	Bxc3 +
8. bxc3	Qf6

WHITE TO MOVE

Solution: The neat winning move is **9. Bh6!.** If Black trades queens, White's bishop corners the rook. Meanwhile, White threatens to give mate at f8 and to trade queens on f6, followed by a bishop fork on g7. Black must lose material.

Comment: When you develop a bishop early, you unprotect the knight pawn the bishop originally guarded. It's not unusual for the enemy queen to zero in on this weakness.

Related Zap: 1. e4 e5 2. d4 exd4 3. c3 dxc3 4. Nxc3 Bb4 5. Qd4 Nc6 6. Qxg7 Bxc3 + 7. bxc3 Qf6 8. Bh6 (Goring Gambit).

Related Zap: 1. e4 e5 2. Nc3 Nc6 3. Bc4 d6 4. Bd5 Qg5 5. Bxc6 + bxc6 6. d3 Qxg2 7. Qf3 Bh3 (Vienna Game).

SICILIAN DEFENSE 19

Overload

1. e4	c5
2. d4	cxd4
3. c3	dxc3
4. Nxc3	d6
5. Bc4	Nf6?
6. e5!	dxe5?

WHITE TO MOVE

Solution: Black just worsened his bad game. With **7. Bxf7+!**, White deflects the Black king to f7 and wins the queen: **7. . . . Kxf7 8. Qxd8.**

Comment: Black's fifth move is too adventurous. Safer is 5. . . . e6, guarding d5 and blocking the a2-f7 diagonal. Generally, don't allow the position to open when your king is in the center and your opponent is better developed.

Related Zap: 1. d4 d5 2. c4 dxc4 3. Nf3 c5 4. e3 cxd4 5. Bxc4 dxe3? 6. Bxf7+ Kxf7 7. Qxd8 (Queen's Gambit Accepted).

SICILIAN DEFENSE **20**

Removing the Guard

1. e4	c5
2. d4	cxd4
3. c3	dxc3
4. Nxc3	d6
5. Bc4	Nf6
6. e5	Ng4
7. e6	Bxe6?

WHITE TO MOVE

Solution: This is a linear case of removing the guard and thereby gaining a piece: **8. Bxe6 fxe6 9. Qxg4.**

Comment: In the Sicilian, when White's king bishop perches on c4, it's wisest for Black to block the bishop's diagonal by moving the king pawn to e6. This tends to blunt White's offensive.

Related Zap: 1. c4 e5 2. d3 Bc5 3. Nf3 d6 4. g3 f5 5. Bg2 e4 6. Ng5 e3 7. Bxe3 Bxe3 8. fxe3 Qxg5 (English Opening).

SICILIAN DEFENSE **21**

Mating Net

1. e4	c5
2. d4	cxd4
3. c3	dxc3
4. Nxc3	Nc6
5. Nf3	d6
6. Bc4	Nf6
7. e5	dxe5
8. Qxd8+	Nxd8
9. Nb5	Kd7?

WHITE TO MOVE

Solution: Trying to prevent a knight fork, Black walks into mate: **10. Nxe5+ Ke8 11. Nc7++**.

Comment: Don't let your guard down once the queens come off the board. With the queens exchanged, certain weaknesses may be harder to defend, such as the square c7 in this example.

Related Zap: 1. e4 e5 2. Nf3 Nc6 3. d4 d6 4. Nc3 Nge7 5. dxe5 dxe5 6. Qxd8+ Kxd8 7. Ng5 Ke8 8. Bc4 Nd8 9. Nb5 Bd7 10. Nxc7++ (Scotch Game).

Related Zap: 1. e4 e5 2. d4 d6 3. dxe5 dxe5 4. Qxd8+ Kxd8 5. Bc4 Ke8 6. Nf3 Nd7 7. Nc3 Ne7 8. Ng5 f6 9. Bf7+ Kd8 10. Ne6++ (Center Game).

Removing the Guard

1. e4	c5
2. d4	cxd4
3. c3	dxc3
4. Nxc3	Nc6
5. Nf3	d6
6. Bc4	Nf6
7. e5	dxe5
8. Qxd8+	Nxd8
9. Nb5	Ne6?

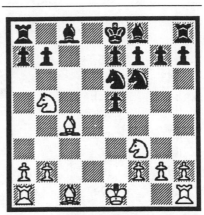

WHITE TO MOVE

Solution: After the immediate **10. Bxe6,** Black can't take back on e6 and prevent the knight fork on c7.

Comment: Black obviously blunders, but in principle, don't rely on a defender that can be captured or driven away.

Related Zap: 1. c4 d6 2. d4 e5 3. dxe5 dxe5 4. Qxd8+ Kxd8 5. a3 Be7 6. Nf3 e4 7. Ne5 Nh6 8. Bxh6 gxh6 9. Nxf7+ (English Opening).

SICILIAN DEFENSE **23**

Pin

1.	e4	c5
2.	Nf3	a6
3.	b4	cxb4
4.	d4	Nf6
5.	e5	Nd5
6.	Ng5	e6
7.	Bd3	h6?
8.	Qh5	Qe7

WHITE TO MOVE

Solution: The immediate **9. Nxf7!** demolishes Black's position. If 9. . . . Qxf7, then 10. Bg6 pins the queen. Otherwise, Black's king rook is pig food.

Comment: The advance of the h-pawn not only weakens g6, it also fails to chase the knight (thanks to 8. Qh5). Many a loss can be attributed to this kind of biteless pawn move.

Related Zap: 1. d4 d5 2. c4 Nf6 3. cxd5 Qxd5 4. Nc3 Qd8 5. e4 e6 6. e5 Nd5 7. Nf3 Nd7 8. Bd3 c6 9. Ng5 h6 10. Qh5 Qe7 11. Nxf7 Qxf7 12. Bg6 (Queen's Gambit Declined).

24

Removing the Guard

1. e4	c5
2. Nf3	g6
3. Bb5	Bg7
4 d3?	

BLACK TO MOVE

Solution: Black wins the misplaced bishop with **4. . . . Qa5+ 5. Nc3 Bxc3+ 6. bxc3 Qxb5.**

Comment: White's bishop development is illogical. It threatens nothing and places the bishop in a vulnerable situation. Instead of moving the d-pawn one square, White should castle.

Related Zap: 1. d4 Nf6 2. c4 e6 3. Nc3 Bb4 4. g3 d5 5. Bg2 dxc4 6. Qa4+ Nc6 7. Bxc6+ bxc6 8. Qxb4 (Nimzo-Indian Defense).

Double Threat

1. e4	c5
2. Nf3	g6
3. c3	b6
4. d4	Bb7
5. Bc4	d5
6. exd5	Bxd5
7. Qa4 +	Bc6?

WHITE TO MOVE

Solution: White wins at least a piece by **8. Ne5!,** threatening the bishop at c6 and mate at f7. If 8. . . . Qc7, then 9. Nxc6 Nxc6 (or 9. . . . Qxc6 10. Bb5) 10. d5.

Comment: Black's play is a little mixed up, starting on the king-side and shifting to the queenside, and then, with the king uncastled, opening the center. That's asking for it.

SICILIAN DEFENSE 26

Fork

1. e4	c5
2. Nf3	e6
3. d4	cxd4
4. Nxd4	a6
5. Bf4?	

BLACK TO MOVE

Solution: Black wins a piece with the fork **5. ... e5!**. After **6. Bxe5**, a second fork, **6. ... Qa5 +**, picks up the undefended bishop.

Comment: With the bishop at f4, White thinks it controls e5 and stops the advance e6-e5. But White overlooks the forking queen check.

Related Zap: 1. d4 Nf6 2. Nf3 c5 3. Bf4 cxd4 4. Nxd4 e5 5. Bxe5 Qa5 + (Queen Pawn Game).

SICILIAN DEFENSE **27**

Discovery

1. e4   c5
2. Nf3   e6
3. d4   cxd4
4. Nxd4   a6
5. Nc3   Bc5
6. Be3   Nf6?

WHITE TO MOVE

Solution: A pawn is expropriated by **7. Nxe6!**. White loses the knight but gains the c5-bishop!

Comment: A case of perfunctory development. Instead of responding to White's threat (to move the knight with a discovered attack on the c5-bishop), Black just makes a move.

Related Zap: 1. e4 e5 2. Nf3 Nc6 3. d4 exd4 4. Nxd4 Bc5 5. Be3 Nf6 6. Nxc6 bxc6. 7. Bxc5 (Scotch Game).

Mating Net

1. e4	c5
2. Nf3	e6
3. d4	cxd4
4. Nxd4	a6
5. Nc3	b5
6. Bd3	Qc7
7. 0-0	d6
8. Bg5	Nbd7
9. e5	dxe5?
10. Nxe6!	fxe6?

WHITE TO MOVE

Solution: One move, **11. Qh5 +,** wins in either of two ways. After 11. . . . g6, either 12. Bxg6 + or 12. Qxg6 + mates next move.

Comment: Black can avoid this mess by capturing on e5 with the knight on move nine. After 9. . . . Nxe5, the c8-bishop defends e6, discouraging a sacrifice.

Related Zap: 1. d4 Nf6 2. c4 e6 3. Nc3 Bb4 4. Bd2 b6 5. a3 Bd6 6. e3 Ba6 7. f3 Nd5 8. cxd5 Qh4 + 9. g3 Qxg3 + 10. hxg3 Bxg3 + + (Nimzo-Indian Defense).

SICILIAN DEFENSE 29

Fork

1. e4	c5
2. Nf3	e6
3. d4	cxd4
4. Nxd4	Nf6
5. e5?	

WHITE TO MOVE

Solution: Black punishes White's audacity with **6. . . . Qa5 +**, winning the e5-pawn.

Comment: In many Sicilians, Black needn't guard against the push e4-e5 because of the forking queen check at a5. The advance tends to become more of a threat after White has developed the queen knight to c3, obstructing the a5-e1 diagonal.

Related Zap: 1. c4 e5 2. d3 Nf6 3. Nf3 Nc6 4. Nxe5 Qa5 + (English Opening).

SICILIAN DEFENSE 30
Trapping

1. e4	c5
2. Nf3	e6
3. d4	cxd4
4. Nxd4	Nf6
5. Nc3	Bb4
6. e5	Nd5
7. Qg4	g6
8. a3	Qa5?

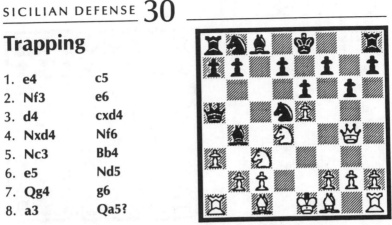

WHITE TO MOVE

Solution: The pin on White's a-pawn fails to the simple **9. axb4! Qxa1 10. Nb3!,** when the queen is trapped and lost, surrounded by little white things.

Comment: When you create a pin on an enemy piece, you must consider, no matter how unlikely it seems, what would happen if the pinned unit moved away. Because, under the right circumstances, it might do just that.

SICILIAN DEFENSE 31

Jettison

1. e4	c5
2. Nf3	Nc6
3. d4	e6?
4. d5	exd5
5. exd5	Nce7
6. Ne5	d6?

WHITE TO MOVE

Solution: A piece is gained by **7. Bb5+**. Since blocking at d7 loses the queen, Black must abandon a knight, **7. . . . Nc6**, permitting **8. dxc6**.

Comment: Black wants to drive away the intrusive knight, but he has to unclog his position as well. Black should offer to exchange off the invader by **6. . . . Ng6**.

Related Zap: 1. d4 d5 2. c4 e6 3. Nc3 Nf6 4. cxd5 Nxd5 5. Nxd5 exd5 6. Bf4 g5 7. Be5 Bb4+ (Queen's Gambit Declined).

Discovery

1. e4	c5
2. Nf3	Nc6
3. d4	cxd4
4. Nxd4	g6
5. Nc3	Bg7
6. Be3	Nf6
7. Bc4	Qa5
8. Qd2?	

BLACK TO MOVE

Solution: Black purloins a pawn by **8. ... Nxe4!**. If **9. Nxe4,** then **9. ... Qxd2+ 10. Kxd2 Nxd4** lets Black keep the material edge. If **9. Nxc6** instead, then **9. ... Qxc3!** insures that Black stays at least a pawn ahead.

Comment: Black often has deadly discoveries along the a1-h8 diagonal after flanking the king bishop. The bishop's fury can be unveiled (by moving the f6-knight) whenever d4 or c3 is vulnerable.

Related Zap: 1. c4 e5 2. Nc3 Nf6 3. Nf3 Nc6 4. g3 d5 5. cxd5 Nxd5 6. Bg2 Be7 7. Nxe5 Nxc3 8. Bxc6+ bxc6 9. dxc3 (English Opening).

SICILIAN DEFENSE 33

Mating Net

1. e4	c5
2. Nf3	Nc6
3. d4	cxd4
4. Nxd4	Nf6
5. Nc3	g6
6. Be3	Bg7
7. Bc4	0-0
8. Bb3	Na5
9. e5	Ne8
10. Bxf7+!	Kxf7
11. Ne6!	Kxe6

WHITE TO MOVE

Solution: White mates with **12. Qd5+ Kf5 13. g4+ Kxg4 14. Rg1+.** If 14. . . . Kh3, then 15. Qg2+ Kh4 16. Qg4++; if 14. . . . Kh4, then 15. Qe4+ Rf4 16. Qxf4+ and mate next move; if 14. . . . Kf5, then 15. Rg5++; finally, if 14. . . . Kh5, then 15. Qd1+ Rf3 16. Qxf3+ Kh4 17. Qg4++.

Comment: Bobby Fischer once played this trap against Sammy Reshevsky, who surrendered his queen but eventually lost anyway.

Discovery

1. e4	c5
2. Nf3	Nc6
3. d4	cxd4
4. Nxd4	Nf6
5. Nc3	d6
6. Bc4	e6
7. 0-0	Be7
8. Be3	0-0
9. g4	h6
10. Bb3	Nxd4
11. Bxd4	

BLACK TO MOVE

Solution: The advance **11. . . . e5** gains time on the bishop to win the g-pawn.

Comment: The advance g2-g4 here is brash. It's risky to move pawns in front of your castled king without sure purpose. The best way to exploit flawed wing attacks is to counter in the center. Hit back in the underbelly.

Related Zap: 1. e4 e5 2. Bc4 Bc5 3. Qg4 g6 4. d3 d5 (Bishop's Opening).

SICILIAN DEFENSE **35**

Double Threat

1. e4	c5
2. Nf3	Nc6
3. d4	cxd4
4. Nxd4	Nf6
5. Nc3	d6
6. Bg5	e6
7. Nxc6	bxc6
8. g3	Rb8
9. Bg2	Rxb2
10. e5	dxe5?

WHITE TO MOVE

Solution: White wins with **11. Qxd8+ Kxd8 12. 0-0-0+!**.

Comment: It's perfectly legal to castle in the above situation. The rules prevent the king, not the rook, from passing through check. Here, the king doesn't violate any rules.

Related Zap: 1. e4 e5 2. Nf3 Nc6 3. Bb5 a6 4. Ba4 d6 5. Bxc6+ bxc6 6. d4 f6 7. Nc3 Rb8 8. Qd3 Ne7 9. Be3 Rxb2 10. dxe5 dxe5 11. Qxd8+ Kxd8 12. 0-0-0+ (Ruy Lopez).

Pin

1. e4	c5
2. Nf3	Nc6
3. d4	cxd4
4. Nxd4	e6
5. Be2	a6
6. 0-0	Qc7
7. f4?	

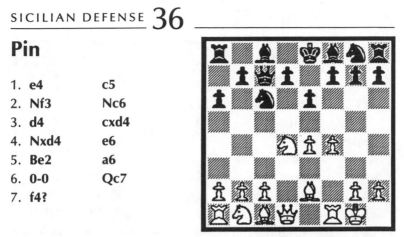

BLACK TO MOVE

Solution: Black wins a knight by **7. . . . Nxd4.** If **8. Qxd4,** then **8. . . . Bc5** pins the queen.

Comment: There are two ways to prepare the advance of the f-pawn while avoiding pinning tactics along the a7-g1 diagonal. You can first develop the bishop to e3, strengthening the vulnerable diagonal; or you can move the king to h1. White, having done neither, drops a knight.

Related Zap: 1. d4 f5 2. c4 g6 3. Nc3 Bg7 4. e3 Nf6 5. Bd2 0-0 6. Rc1 d5 7. cxd5 Nxd5 8. Nxd5 Qxd5 9. Bc4 (Dutch Defense).

SICILIAN DEFENSE 37

Fork

1. e4	c5
2. Nf3	Nc6
3. d4	cxd4
4. Nxd4	e6
5. Nc3	a6
6. Be3	Qc7
7. Nxc6	Qxc6
8. Bd4	f6
9. Bd3	Bc5?

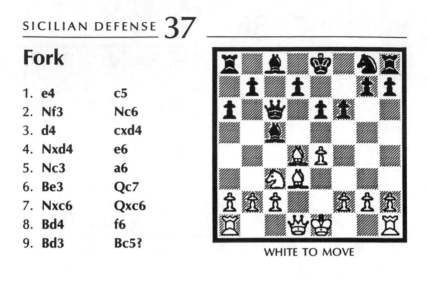

WHITE TO MOVE

Solution: White forks king and bishop, **10. Qh5+**, pilfering the bishop.

Comment: A red flag should go up in White's mind when Black's king is still on its original square and the f-pawn moves to f6. If Black's bishop goes to c5, White might be able to win the bishop with a queen check at h5.

Related Zap: 1. e4 e5 2. Nf3 Nc6 3. Bb5 a6 4. Bxc6 dxc6 5. 0-0 f6 6. d4 exd4 7. Nxd4 Bc5 8. Qh5+ (Ruy Lopez).

Overload

1. e4	c5
2. Nf3	Nc6
3. d4	cxd4
4. Nxd4	e6
5. Nc3	a6
6. Be3	Qc7
7. Qd2	b5
8. 0-0-0	Bb7
9. Nb3	Rc8?

WHITE TO MOVE

Solution: The shot **10. Bb6!** wins a piece. Black can't take the bishop or move the queen to safety without allowing mate at d7.

Comment: Black's ninth move, trying to use the half-open c-file, is a natural mistake. The problem can be avoided by first playing d7-d6, protecting the d-pawn.

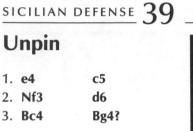

SICILIAN DEFENSE **39**

Unpin

1. e4   c5
2. Nf3   d6
3. Bc4   Bg4?

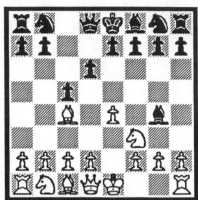

WHITE TO MOVE

Solution: White wins a pawn with **4. Bxf7 +! Kxf7 5. Ng5 +,** followed by capturing the bishop with the queen.

Comment: Early pins by Black's queen bishop are often premature and subject to pin-breaking sacrifices. Here, Black pins for the sake of pinning, without considering the needs of the position.

Related Zap: 1. e4 e5 2. f4 d6 3. Nf3 Bg4 4. Bc4 Be7 5. fxe5 dxe5 6. Bxf7 + Kxf7 7. Nxe5 + (King's Gambit Declined).

40

Overload

1. e4	c5
2. Nf3	d6
3. g3	Nc6
4. Bg2	Bg4
5. 0-0	Nd4
6. h3?	

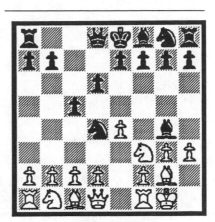

BLACK TO MOVE

Solution: Black wins a pawn by **6. . . . Nxf3+ 7. Bxf3 Bxh3.**

Comment: White's sixth move is a typical error (6. c3 is better). The g2-bishop is overworked. It can't come to the aid of f3 without abandoning h3.

Related Zap: 1. e4 e5 2. Nf3 Nc6 3. Bc4 Bc5 4. Nc3 Nc6 5. d3 d6 6. Bg5 0-0 7. Nd5 h6 8. Nxf6+ gxf6 9. Bxh6 (Giuoco Piano).

Overload

1. e4	c5
2. Nf3	d6
3. Bb5+	Nd7
4. d4	Nf6
5. Bxd7+	Nxd7
6. Nc3	e6
7. Bg5	Qc7
8. 0-0	cxd4
9. Nxd4	h6?
10. Nxe6!	fxe6?

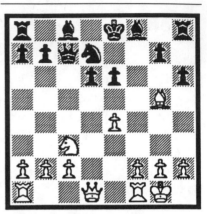

WHITE TO MOVE

Solution: It's mate: **11. Qh5+ g6 12. Qxg6++.**

Comment: Bad pawn moves create weaknesses. Here, the advance of Black's rook pawn weakens g6. White sacrifices the knight on e6 to draw away the f-pawn, and Black has no defense to the queen check at h5.

Related Zap: 1. f4 e6 2. h3 Qh4+ 3. g3 Qxg3++ (Bird's Opening).

Related Zap: 1. d4 f5 2. e4 fxe4 3. f3 exf3 4. Bd3 fxg2 5. Qh5+ g6 6. Qxg6+ hxg6 7. Bxg6++ (Dutch Defense).

Related Zap: 1. d4 d6 2. Nf3 Bg4 3. h3 Bxf3 4. gxf3 Nf6 5. Nd2 e6 6. b3 Nd5 7. c4 Ne3 8. fxe3 Qh4++ (Queen Pawn Game).

42

Unpin

1. e4	c5
2. Nf3	d6
3. c3	Nc6
4. d4	Bg4
5. d5	Ne5?

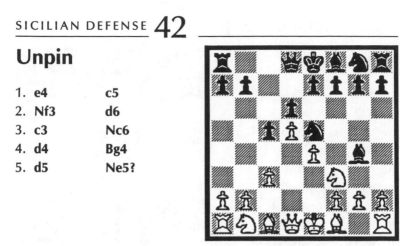

WHITE TO MOVE

Solution: White shows the pin to be illusory with **6. Nxe5! Bxd1 7. Bb5 +,** when Black must give back the queen and more.

Comment: Black relies too heavily on his queenside forces and the pin of the f3-knight. After move five, none of Black's eight kingside units have moved—a bad sign.

Related Zap: 1. d4 d5 2. c4 e6 3. Nc3 Nf6 4. Bf4 c5 5. Nb5 cxd4 6. Nc7+ Qxc7 7. Bxc7 Bb4+ 8. Qd2 Bxd2+ 9. Kxd2 dxc4 (Queen's Gambit Declined).

SICILIAN DEFENSE 43

Unpin

1. e4	c5
2. Nf3	d6
3. c3	Nc6
4. d4	cxd4
5. cxd4	Bg4
6. d5	Ne5?
7. Nxe5!	Qa5 +
8. Bd2	Bxd1
9. Bxa5	dxe5?

WHITE TO MOVE

Solution: White could stay a piece ahead by taking the bishop, but nothing is quite as good as **10. Bb5 mate!**

Comment: The position is lost after Black's sixth move, when 7. Nxe5! Bxd1 8. Bb5+ regains the queen with interest. Live by the pin, but don't die by it.

Related Zap: 1. d4 d5 2. Bg5 c5 3. e3 Qc7 4. Nf3 Bg4 5. Nbd2 Nc6 6. c3 e5 7. dxe5 Nxe5 8. Nxe5 Bxd1 9. Bb5 + (Queen Pawn Game).

SICILIAN DEFENSE 44

Jettison

1. e4	c5
2. Nf3	d6
3. d4	b6?
4. dxc5	bxc5?

WHITE TO MOVE

Solution: Don't expect to survive if you make several weakening pawn moves in the opening. White wins a piece with **5. Qd5,** when to save a rook Black must ditch a knight: **5. . . . Nc6 6. Qxc6+ Bd7.**

Comment: Black takes back with the b-pawn to avoid an unfavorable queen trade. But no problems result from exchanging c-pawn for d-pawn on the third move, which is the proper strategy.

Related Zap: 1. d4 d5 2. c4 dxc4 3. e3 b5 4. a4 c6 5. axb5 cxb5 6. Qf3 (Queen's Gambit Accepted).

SICILIAN DEFENSE 45

Jettison

1. **e4**	**c5**
2. **Nf3**	**d6**
3. **d4**	**cxd4**
4. **Nxd4**	**Nf6**
5. **Nc3**	**g6**
6. **Be3**	**Ng4?**

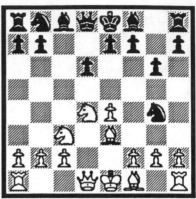

WHITE TO MOVE

Solution: After **7. Bb5 + !**, Black loses material by blocking on c6 or answering **7. . . . Bd7.** The latter loses a knight to **8. Qxg4!**, when the pin on the d7-bishop prevents it from taking White's queen.

Comment: It's a typical error to assume that because something is guarded on one move, it must be guarded on the next. Here, the bishop check ends the knight's protection.

Related Zap: 1. d4 c5 2. d5 d6 3. e4 Nf6 4. Nc3 g6 5. Be3 Ng4 6. Bb5 + Bd7 7. Qxg4 (Benoni Defense).

SICILIAN DEFENSE 46
Discovery

1. e4	c5
2. Nf3	d6
3. d4	cxd4
4. Nxd4	Nf6
5. Nc3	g6
6. Be3	Bg7
7. Bc4	0-0
8. f3	Nc6
9. Qd2	Bd7
10. 0-0-0	Rc8
11. h4?	

BLACK TO MOVE

Solution: Black wins a piece with **11. . . . Nxd4 12. Qxd4 Ng4!** (if 13. Qd3, then 13. . . . Nxe3).

Comment: White can avoid the loss of a piece by retreating the bishop to b3 on move 11. This withdrawal is standard. It removes the bishop from the half-open c-file and avoids potentially menacing pawn spikes at b5 and d5.

Double Threat

1. e4	c5
2. Nf3	d6
3. d4	cxd4
4. Nxd4	Nf6
5. Nc3	a6
6. Bg5	Nbd7
7. Bc4	h6
8. Bxf6	gxf6?

WHITE TO MOVE

Solution: Black loses his queen after **9. Bxf7 + !**. The main line goes **9. . . . Kxf7 10. Qh5 + Kg8 11. Qg6 + Bg7 12. Ne6.**

Comment: With this sixth move, Black tries to avoid doubled pawns, so 8. . . . gxf6 is illogical. Worse: it loses the queen.

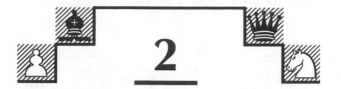

2

ALEKHINE DEFENSE

(TRAPS 48-70)

1. e4 Nf6

TRAPS	WHITE'S 2ND MOVE	BLACK'S 2ND MOVE
48	2. Bc4	2. . . . Nxe4
49	2. d3	2. . . . e5
50	2. d3	2. . . . d5
51	2. Nc3	2. . . . Rg8
52	2. Nc3	2. . . . Nc6
53	2. Nc3	2. . . . g6
54-63	2. Nc3	2. . . . d5
64	2. e5	2. . . . Ne4
65-70	2. e5	2. . . . Nd5

ALEKHINE DEFENSE **48**

Discovery

1. e4	Nf6
2. Bc4	Nxe4
3. Bxf7 +	Kxf7
4. Qh5 +	Kf6
5. Qf3 +	Ke5
6. d4 +	Kxd4
7. Ne2 +	Ke5
8. Bf4 +	Kf5?

WHITE TO MOVE

Solution: White wins the queen with **9. Bxc7 +**.

Comment: I recommend staying away from lines in which six of the first eight moves are made with the king. Even though Black might be able to work his way through this labyrinth with great care, it makes more sense to avoid it altogether by obstructing the c4-bishop. Next time a bishop blatantly occupies c4, block it with e7-e6 and live longer and prosper.

49

Mating Net

1. e4	Nf6
2. d3	e5
3. f4	Bc5
4. fxe5	Nxe4
5. dxe4	Qh4+
6. Ke2?	

BLACK TO MOVE

Solution: Mate follows **6. . . . Qxe4+.** If either 7. Be3 or 7. Kd2, Black ends it by putting the queen on e3.

Comment: White also loses after 6. g3 Qxe4+. But by playing 6. Kd2!, White has a chance to survive the storm. Don't lose heart just because you're under attack. Find ways to keep the game alive and you might turn it around.

Related Zap: 1. e4 e5 2. Nf3 Nc6 3. d4 exd4 4. Nxd4 Nf6 5. f3 Bc5 6. Nb3 Bb6 7. Bb5 0-0 8. a4 Nxe4 9. fxe4 Qh4+ 10. g3 Qxe4+ 11. Kd2 Qe3++ (Scotch Game).

ALEKHINE DEFENSE **50**

Mating Net

1.	e4	Nf6
2.	d3	d5
3.	e5	Nfd7
4.	d4	c5
5.	Bd3	cxd4
6.	e6	fxe6?

WHITE TO MOVE

Solution: After **7. Qh5 + g6,** it is mate by either 8. Bxg6+ hxg6 9. Qxg6+ + or 8. Qxg6+ hxg6 9. Bxg6+ +. Take your pick.

Comment: Instead of taking the e-pawn, Black can stave off mate with 6. . . . Nf6, guarding h5. Though Black loses the right to castle after 7. exf7+ Kxf7, the king has shelter and the center pawns look formidable.

Related Zap: 1. c4 e5 2. Nf3 Bd6 3. d4 e4 4. Nfd2 e3 5. fxe3 Qh4+ 6. g3 Qxg3+ 7. hxg3 Bxg3+ + (English Opening).

ALEKHINE DEFENSE **51**

Trapping

1. e4   Nf6
2. Nc3   Rg8?

WHITE TO MOVE

Solution: White seizes Black's knight with **3. e5!**. Nowhere to run. Nowhere to hide.

Comment: Whether Black was called for "touch move" or made a horrible blunder, this example illustrates how vulnerable a knight can be when it lacks central support, even when occupying a strong square in its own camp, minding its own business.

Related Zap: 1. c4 c6 2. Nc3 d5 3. e3 Nf6 4. cxd5 cxd5 5. Bb5+ Bd7 6. Nge2 a6 7. Bxd7+ Qxd7 8. b4 e5 9. Rb1 d4 (English Opening).

ALEKHINE DEFENSE 52

Trapping

1.	e4	Nf6
2.	Nc3	Nc6
3.	d4	g6
4.	d5	Ne5?

WHITE TO MOVE

Solution: White wins a knight by **5. f4 Neg4 6. e5.**

Comment: I try to dissuade my students from playing around with knights in the center without moving any center pawns. It becomes hard to support the knights and practically impossible to stop menacing pawn advances against them.

Related Zap: 1. e4 Nf6 2. e5 Nd5 3. d4 Nc6 4. c4 Nb6 5. Nc3 g6 6. c5 (Alekhine Defense).

Mating Net

1. e4   Nf6
2. Nc3   g6
3. Nd5   Nxe4
4. Qe2   Nd6?

WHITE TO MOVE

Solution: The mating game is **5. Nf6 + +**.

Comment: Three things occur to allow a smothered mate on f6: the g-pawn moves, the king knight shifts out of position, and the e-pawn becomes pinned. To avoid all this, Black must create weaknesses on move four with f7-f5 or lose a pawn with c7-c6.

Related Zap: 1. e4 c5 2. Nf3 Nf6 3. Nc3 d5 4. Bb5+ Bd7 5. Qe2 dxe4? 6. Nxe4 Nc6 7. Nd6 + + (Sicilian Defense).

ALEKHINE DEFENSE 54

Pin

1.	e4	Nf6
2.	Nc3	d5
3.	e5	Nfd7
4.	d4	c5
5.	Nxd5	cxd4
6.	Qxd4?	

BLACK TO MOVE

Solution: Black pins and wins the d5-knight, **6. . . . Nb6,** for 7. c4 is met by 7. . . . e6.

Comment: The incorrect timing of White's central captures creates problems. Taking on d5 is safe on move four, but on move five it leads to trouble.

55

Fork

1.	e4	Nf6
2.	Nc3	d5
3.	e5	Ne4
4.	Nxe4	dxe4
5.	d4	exd3
6.	Bxd3	Nc6
7.	Qe2	Nd4
8.	Qe4	Bf5
9.	Qxb7	

BLACK TO MOVE

Solution: Black cashes in with **9. . . . Bxd3 10. cxd3 Rb8!**. After **11. Qxa7**, Black forks king and rook, **11. . . . Nc2+**.

Comment: Three queen moves in a row just to win the enemy b-pawn is not a good use of resources, especially when the queen goes so far as to abandon key squares (c2 and d3) to opposing forces.

Fork

1. e4   Nf6
2. Nc3   d5
3. exd5   Nxd5
4. Nf3   Bf5
5. Nxd5   Qxd5
6. d4?

BLACK TO MOVE

Solution: Black pilfers a pawn by **6. . . . Qe4+**, when c2 can't be saved.

Comment: Instead of moving the d-pawn two squares, White should prepare for castling by 6. Be2. This also closes the e-file so that Black's queen can't move to e4 with check to win the c-pawn.

Related Zap: 1. e4 e5 2. Nf3 Nc6 3. Bc4 Nd4 4. Nxe5 Qg5 5. Nxf7 Qxg2 6. Nxh8 Qxe4+ 7. Be2 Nxc2+ 8. Kf1 Qxh1++ (Italian Game).

57

Direct Attack

1.	e4	Nf6
2.	Nc3	d5
3.	exd5	Nxd5
4.	Nge2	Bf5
5.	d4?	

BLACK TO MOVE

Solution: White cannot protect c2 after **5. . . . Nb4!.**

Comment: By advancing the d-pawn to d3 White can stop the bishop's assault on c2. But even better than 5. d3 is 5. Ng3, attacking the bishop. That should slow Black down.

Related Zap: 1. d4 d5 2. Nc3 Nc6 3. Bf4 g6 4. Nb5 (Queen Pawn Game).

ALEKHINE DEFENSE 58
Mating Net

1. e4	Nf6
2. Nc3	d5
3. exd5	Nxd5
4. Nge2	Nc6
5. g3	Bg4
6. Bg2	Nd4
7. Bxd5	Qxd5!
8. Nxd5?	

BLACK TO MOVE

Solution: It's mate in two: **8. . . . Nf3+ 9. Kf1 Bh3++**.

Comment: Black's queen-for-bishop sacrifice destroys White's ability to guard f3 and h3. In the final position, it's those two squares that Black occupies to fashion mate.

Related Zap: 1. e4 e5 2. Nf3 Nc6 3. Bb5 d6 4. d4 Bd7 5. Nc3 Nge7 6. Bc4 exd4 7. Nxd4 g6 8. Bg5 Bg7 9. Nd5 Bxd4 10. Qxd4 Nxd4 11. Nf6+ Kf8 12. Bh6++ (Ruy Lopez).

Related Zap: 1. e4 e5 2. Nf3 Nc6 3. Nc3 g6 4. d4 exd4 5. Nd5 Bg7 6. Bg5 Nge7 7. Nxd4 Bxd4 8. Qxd4 Nxd4 9. Nf6+ Kf8 10. Bh6++ (Three Knights Game).

Mating Net

1. e4	Nf6
2. Nc3	d5
3. exd5	Nxd5
4. Nge2	Nc6
5. g3	Bg4
6. Bg2	Nd4
7. Bxd5	Qxd5
8. 0-0	Nf3 +
9. Kg2	

BLACK TO MOVE

Solution: The game ends thus: **9. . . . Nh4 + 10. Kg1 Qg2 + +.** The same mate results from **9. . . . Ne1 +.**

Comment: Black sets up the mate with a double check. After 9. . . . Nh4 +, both Black's queen and knight are attacked, but neither one can be taken because both give check. White must move the king to g1, and mate follows.

Related Zap: 1. e4 e5 2. f4 exf4 3. Nf3 d5 4. Nc3 dxe4 5. Nxe4 Bg4 6. Qe2 Bxf3 7. Nf6 + + (King's Gambit Accepted).

60

Mating Net

1. e4	Nf6
2. Nc3	d5
3. exd5	Nxd5
4. Nge2	Nc6
5. g3	Bg4
6. Bg2	Nd4
7. Bxd5	Qxd5
8. 0-0	Nf3+
9. Kh1	Ng5+
10. Nxd5	

BLACK TO MOVE

Solution: Black mates by **10. . . . Bf3+ 11. Kg1 Nh3++**.

Comment: White is done in by the weakness of the light squares. If the king bishop were still at g2, it would guard f3 and h3, the two exploited squares. In your own play, once you've fianchettoed your king bishop, try to hold onto it to safeguard your king.

Related Zap: 1. d4 Nf6 2. c4 e6 3. Nc3 Bb4 4. e3 b6 5. Nf3 Bb7 6. Bd3 Ne4 7. Qc2 f5 8. 0-0 Bxc3 9. bxc3 0-0 10. Nd2 Qh4 11. g3 Ng5 12. gxh4 Nh3++ (Nimzo-Indian Defense).

61

Fork

1. e4	Nf6
2. Nc3	d5
3. exd5	Nxd5
4. Bc4	Nxc3
5. bxc3	Nc6
6. d4	Na5?

WHITE TO MOVE

Solution: White has a petite combination: **7. Bxf7+ Kxf7 8. Qh5+**, winning the knight at a5.

Comment: Black falls behind in development by moving the knight for a second time instead of advancing the e-pawn one square, which releases the king bishop and prepares for castling. Even if 6. . . . Na5 didn't lose a pawn, it removes the knight from the center, attacking without building.

Related Zap: 1. d4 d5 2. c4 dxc4 3. e3 Nc6 4. Bxc4 Na5 5. Bxf7+ Kxf7 6. Qh5+ g6 7. Qxa5 (Queen's Gambit Declined).

ALEKHINE DEFENSE **62**

Fork

1. e4	Nf6
2. Nc3	d5
3. exd5	Nxd5
4. Bc4	e6
5. Bxd5	exd5
6. Qe2 +	Be6

WHITE TO MOVE

Solution: White annexes the b-pawn by **7. Qb5 +**.

Comment: Many players are reluctant to exchange bishop for knight early in the game just to win a pawn, particularly if the queen has to move as many as three times. But a pawn has real value, so if trading enables you to win one, consider it.

Related Zap: 1. e4 e6 2. d4 d5 3. exd5 exd5 4. Nf3 Bg4 5. Qe2 + Be7 6. Qb5 + (French Defense).

Related Zap: 1. d4 d5 2. e3 Bf5 3. Bd3 e6 4. Bxf5 exf5 5. Qd3 g6 6. Qb5 + (Queen Pawn Game).

63

Fork

1. e4	Nf6
2. Nc3	d5
3. exd5	Nxd5
4. Bc4	e6
5. Bxd5	exd5
6. Qe2+	Be7

WHITE TO MOVE

Solution: White extracts a pawn by 7. Qe5, forking d5 and g7.

Comment: After 4. Bc4, Black should exchange on c3 or withdraw the knight to b6. After 6. Qe2+, Black hangs the d-pawn (7. Nxd5) if he answers 6. . . . Qe7.

Related Zap: 1. d4 d5 2. Bg5 Qd6 3. Nd2 e5 4. dxe5 Qxe5 (Queen Pawn Game).

ALEKHINE DEFENSE  64

Trapping

1. e4   Nf6
2. e5   Ne4
3. d3   Nc5
4. d4   Ne4?

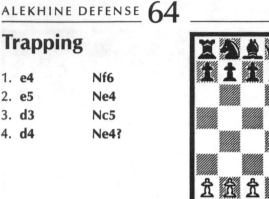

WHITE TO MOVE

Solution: The knight is trapped by **5. f3.**

Comment: Black's knight, with no visible support, is encircled by opposing pawns in the middle of the board. It's the only thing Black moves, and the only thing Black loses.

Related Zap: 1. e4 Nf6 2. e5 Ne4 3. b4 Nc6 4. d3 (Alekhine Defense).

ALEKHINE DEFENSE 65

Overload

1. e4	Nf6
2. e5	Nd5
3. Nc3	Nxc3
4. dxc3	d6
5. Bc4	dxe5?

WHITE TO MOVE

Solution: The shot **6. Bxf7 +!** deflects the king from the defense of the queen. White's queen then takes Black's.

Comment: White takes away from the center (4. dxc3) to facilitate development and open lines. Indeed, White's slightly better development and ability to use the d-file set up the win.

Related Zap: 1. e4 e5 2. d4 exd4 3. c3 dxc3 4. Bc4 cxb2 5. Bxb2 d6 6. Nc3 Nf6 7. e5 dxe5 8. Bxf7 + Ke7 9. Ba3 + Kxf7 10. Qxd8 (Danish Gambit).

Related Zap: 1. d4 d5 2. c4 e6 3. Nf3 c5 4. dxc5 Bxc5 5. cxd5 Nf6 6. dxe6 Bxf2 + 7. Kxf2 Qxd1 (Queen's Gambit Declined)

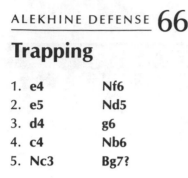

ALEKHINE DEFENSE **66**

Trapping

1. e4	Nf6
2. e5	Nd5
3. d4	g6
4. c4	Nb6
5. Nc3	Bg7?

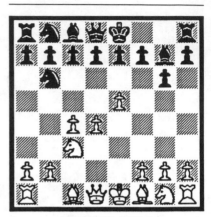

WHITE TO MOVE

Solution: Push the c-pawn and win a knight, **6. c5.**

Comment: If you surrender the center without an intelligent fight, you will have few possibilities and your opponent will have many. Black's lonesome knight becomes squashed plant meal before White's central juggernaut.

Related Zap: 1. d4 Nc6 2. d5 Ne5 3. f4 Ng6 4. Nf3 Nf6 5. f5 (Queen Pawn Game).

67

Pin

1. e4	Nf6
2. e5	Nd5
3. d4	d6
4. c4	Nb6
5. exd6	cxd6
6. Nc3	Bf5
7. Qf3	Qd7
8. c5!	dxc5

WHITE TO MOVE

Solution: White garners a piece with **9. Bb5! Nc6 10. d5.**

Comment: Black misses the point behind advancing the c-pawn to c5: it's to clear the a6-f1 diagonal for the king bishop to go to b5. Instead of 8. . . . dxc5, Black can breathe a little longer by first attacking White's queen, 8. . . . Bg4. He needs to gain time to rescue his various threatened and burdened pieces (b6-knight, f5-bishop, and queen).

Related Zap: 1. e4 e5 2. Nf3 Nc6 3. Nc3 Nf6 4. Bb5 d6 5. 0-0 Qd7 6. Nd5 Nxd5 7. exd5 a6 8. dxc6 (Four Knights Game).

ALEKHINE DEFENSE 68

Pin

1. e4	Nf6
2. e5	Nd5
3. d4	d6
4. Nf3	Bg4
5. Be2	Bxf3
6. Bxf3	dxe5

WHITE TO MOVE

Solution: White wins the exchange by **7. c4!**. Once the knight moves, the bishop captures on b7 and then on a8.

Comment: After Black takes back on e5, it's natural to expect White to take back. But the surprising **7. c4!** exploits Black's weakened b7, made vulnerable by the early development of the c8-bishop.

Mating Net

1. e4	Nf6
2. e5	Nd5
3. d4	d6
4. Nf3	Bg4
5. Bc4	Nb6
6. Bb3	dxe5
7. Nxe5	Bxd1

WHITE TO MOVE

Solution: It's immediate mate: **8. Bxf7.**

Comment: Black shouldn't take White's queen, but there aren't great alternatives. If 7. . . . Be6, White is on top after 8. Bxe6 fxe6 9. Qh5+ g6 10. Nxg6.

Related Zap: 1. d4 Nf6 2. c4 e5 3. d5 Bc5 4. Bg5 Ne4 5. Bxd8 Bxf2++ (Budapest Defense).

ALEKHINE DEFENSE **70**

Mating Net

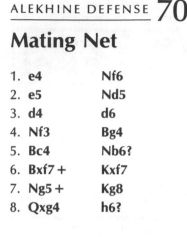

1. e4	Nf6
2. e5	Nd5
3. d4	d6
4. Nf3	Bg4
5. Bc4	Nb6?
6. Bxf7+	Kxf7
7. Ng5+	Kg8
8. Qxg4	h6?

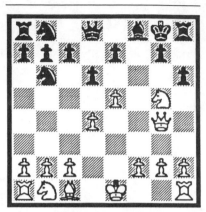

WHITE TO MOVE

Solution: The queen gives diagonal mate, **9. Qe6++**.

Comment: By his eighth move, Black is definitely lost, but it isn't necessary to lose in one move. Instead of 8. . . . h6?, Black could delay matters with 8. . . . Qc8 or even 8. . . . Qd7.

Related Zap: 1. e4 e5 2. Nc3 Nf6 3. Bc4 Nxe4 4. Bxf7+ Kxf7 5. Nxe4 d5 6. Qf3+ Kg8 7. Ng5 Qxg5 8. Qxd5+ Be6 9. Qxe6++ (Vienna Game).

Related Zap: 1. e4 c5 2. Nf3 Nf6 3. e5 Nd5 4. Bc4 Nb6 5. Bxf7+ Kxf7 6. Ng5+ Kg8 7. Qf3 Qe8 8. e6 h6 9. Qf7+ Qxf7 10. exf7++ (Sicilian Defense).

3

CARO-KANN DEFENSE
(TRAPS 71-111)

1. e4 c6

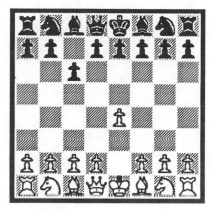

TRAPS	WHITE'S 2ND MOVE	BLACK'S 2ND MOVE
71-72	2. d3	2. . . . d5
73	2. c4	2. . . . d5
74-75	2. c4	2. . . . e5
76-81	2. Nc3	2. . . . d5
82	2. d4	2. . . . Na6
83	2. d4	2. . . . d6
84-111	2. d4	2. . . . d5

continued

	WHITE'S 3D MOVE	BLACK'S 3D MOVE
84	3. Bd3	3. . . . Nf6
85	3. Bd3	3. . . . e6
86	3. Bd3	3. . . . dxe4
87	3. e5	3. . . . f6
88	3. e5	3. . . . e6
89-92	3. e5	3. . . . Bf5
93-98	3. exd5	3. . . . cxd5
99-111	3. Nc3	3. . . . dxe4

CARO-KANN DEFENSE 71

Fork

1. e4	c6
2. d3	d5
3. Nc3	e5
4. Nf3	Nf6
5. Nxe5?	d4
6. Ne2	

BLACK TO MOVE

Solution: White has bitten off more than he can chew. With **6. . . . Qa5 +**, Black's queen forks king and knight.

Comment: The forking queen check may not seem possible immediately after White's knight takes the e-pawn, with the d5-pawn obstructing the fifth rank and the c3-knight blocking the a5-e1 diagonal. But a single pawn move clears the attacking lanes.

Related Zap: 1. e4 c5 2. Nf3 d6 3. c3 Nc6 4. d4 Nf6 5. Be2 Nxe4 6. d5 Ne5 7. Qa4+ (Sicilian Defense).

CARO-KANN DEFENSE 72

Discovery

1. e4	c6
2. d3	d5
3. Nc3	e5
4. Nf3	Nf6
5. exd5	cxd5
6. Nxe5	d4
7. Qe2	dxc3

WHITE TO MOVE

Solution: White wins the queen with a vicious discovered check, **8. Nc6+**.

Comment: Black plays in a vacuum. When White seems to ignore the threat to the knight on c3, Black blindly takes it without considering the consequences. That's how chess games are lost.

Related Zap: 1. e4 e5 2. Nf3 Nf6 3. Nxe5 Nxe4 4. Qe2 Nf6 5. Nc6+ (Petrov Defense).

CARO-KANN DEFENSE **73**

Discovery

1. e4	c6
2. c4	d5
3. exd5	cxd5
4. cxd5	Nf6
5. Qa4+	Bd7
6. Qb3	Na6
7. Qxb7	Nc5
8. Qb4	e6
9. dxe6?	

BLACK TO MOVE

Solution: It's curtains for the queen after **9.... Nd3+!** **10. Bxd3 Bxb4.** White cuts his losses by **11. exd7+ Qxd7.**

Comment: An example of queen overuse. The queen checks (5. Qa4+) to draw out Black's bishop (5. . . . Bd7) and weaken the b-pawn. White shifts the attack to the b-pawn (6. Qb3). Black lets the pawn hang, using the time to make two useful moves with the knight. White holds the pawn, but loses the queen.

Related Zap: 1. Nf3 d5 2. g3 Nf6 3. Bg2 Bf5 4. c4 e6 5. cxd5 exd5 6. Qb3 Nbd7 7. Qxb7 Nc5 8. Qb5+ c6 9. Qb4 Nd3+ (Reti Opening).

Interference

1. e4	c6
2. c4	e5
3. Nf3	Qa5
4. Be2	f5
5. exf5	e4
6. Ng5	Qxf5
7. d3	Bb4 +
8. Bd2?	

BLACK TO MOVE

Solution: Black cuts the knight's defense by **8. . . . e3!**, when **9. Bxb4?** falls to **9. . . . Qxf2 + +.** (On 9. fxe3, Black wins the knight: 9. . . . Bxd2 + and 10. . . . Qxg5.)

Comment: White's d2-bishop proves to be overloaded. It can't take on e3 to keep the g5-knight protected because it's pinned to the king.

Related Zap: 1. d4 d5 2. c4 e5 3. dxe5 d4 4. e3 Bb4 + 5. Bd2 dxe3 6. Bxb4 exf2 + 7. Ke2 fxg1(N) + 8. Rxg1 Bg4 + (Albin Counter Gambit).

Fork

1. e4	c6
2. c4	e5
3. Nf3	Qa5
4. Be2	f5
5. exf5	e4
6. Ng5	Qxf5
7. d3	d5
8. cxd5	cxd5
9. dxe4	dxe4

WHITE TO MOVE

Solution: White depletes Black's arsenal by a pawn after the forking queen check, **10. Qa4 +**. It's downhill from there.

Comment: Black develops only one piece in the first nine moves—the queen—and moves it twice. The other seven moves are with pawns. This is not a judicious use of one's forces.

Related Zap: 1. e4 d6 2. Nf3 Nf6 3. c3 Nxe4 4. Qa4+ (Pirc Defense).

CARO-KANN DEFENSE **76**

Jettison

1. e4	c6
2. Nc3	d5
3. exd5	cxd5
4. Nf3	Bg4
5. h3	Bh5
6. g4	Bg6
7. Ne5	d4?

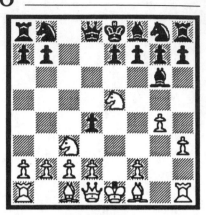

WHITE TO MOVE

Solution: After **8. Bb5 +,** the queen knight must be jettisoned on c6.

Comment: After being driven to h5, Black's bishop is not in position to block checks along the a4-e8 diagonal. With Black's c-pawn gone, and White's knight controlling c6 and d7, the bishop check at b5 is crushing.

Related Zap: 1. e4 c5 2. c3 e6 3. d4 Nf6 4. e5 Nd5 5. Nf3 f5 6. Be2 Nc6 7. c4 Nb6 8. d5 Ne7 9. d6 Ng6 10. Bg5 (Sicilian Defense).

Pin

1. e4	c6
2. Nc3	d5
3. Qf3	dxe4
4. Nxe4	Nf6
5. Nxf6 +	gxf6
6. Bc4	Nd7
7. Qh5	Ne5
8. Bb3	Qa5?

WHITE TO MOVE

Solution: White wins the knight with **9. Bxf7 + ! Kd8** (taking the bishop, 9. . . . Nxf7, loses the queen, 10. Qxa5) **10. f4 Nc4 11. Qxa5 + Nxa5 12. b4.**

Comment: Black threatens 9. . . . Nd3 +, uncovering an attack to White's queen. But the threat rebounds, for Black's knight is pinned to its own queen and can't safely recapture on f7. The trapper gets trapped.

Related Zap: 1. d4 f5 2. e4 fxe4 3. Nc3 Nf6 4. Bg5 c5 5. Bxf6 exf6 6. Bc4 cxd4 7. Nd5 Qa5 + 8. c3 dxc3 9. Qh5 + g6 10. Nxf6 + Ke7 11. Qxa5 (Dutch Defense).

CARO-KANN DEFENSE 78

Fork

1. e4	c6
2. Nc3	d5
3. Qf3	dxe4
4. Nxe4	Nd7
5. d4	Ngf6
6. Bc4	e6
7. Bg5	Be7
8. h4	Nxe4
9. Bxe7?	

BLACK TO MOVE

Solution: Black gains a piece by **9. . . . Qxe7 10. Qxe4 Qb4 +**.

Comment: White should merely recapture the knight (9. Qxe4). Interposing another exchange (9. Bxe7?) lets the Black queen set up a shot. White can't defend adequately because Black's knight on e4 has not been recaptured. Generally, if a unit of yours is taken, take back before doing anything else.

Related Zap: 1. d4 d5 2. c4 e6 3. Nc3 Nf6 4. Bg5 Be7 5. e3 Ne4 6. Bxe7 Qxe7 7. Bd3 Nxc3 8. bxc3 c5 9. Ne2 cxd4 10. cxd4 dxc4 11. Bxc4 Qb4 + (Queen's Gambit Declined).

CARO-KANN DEFENSE 79
Overload

1. e4	c6
2. Nc3	d5
3. Nf3	d4
4. Nb1	f6
5. Bc4	Bg4?
6. Ne5!	fxe5
7. Qxg4	Qd6?

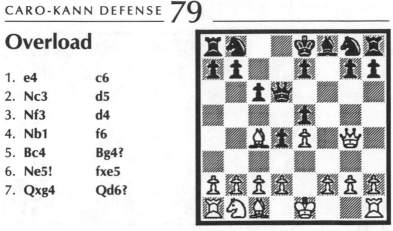

WHITE TO MOVE

Solution: Black develops the queen, only to lose it: **8. Qc8 + Qd8 9. Bf7 +! Kxf7 10. Qxd8.**

Comment: Black makes several questionable moves. Advancing the f-pawn weakens Black's position and wastes time. Developing the queen bishop is premature. Defending with the queen fails. That's enough to lose most chess games.

Related Zap: 1. d4 d5 2. c4 e6 3. Nf3 c5 4. dxc5 Bxc5 5. Nbd2 dxc4 6. Nxc4 Bxf2 + 7. Kxf2 Qxd1 (Queen's Gambit Declined).

CARO-KANN DEFENSE **80**

Mating Net

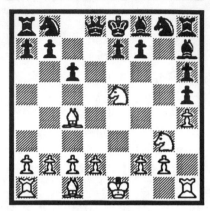

1.	e4	c6
2.	Nc3	d5
3.	Nf3	dxe4
4.	Nxe4	Bf5
5.	Ng3	Bg6
6.	h4	h6
7.	Ne5	Bh7
8.	Qh5	g6
9.	Bc4	gxh5?

WHITE TO MOVE

Solution: It's mate in one: **10. Bxf7 + +.**

Comment: Black is forced to waste a few tempi (three moves for the bishop to reach h7, and two moves for the g-pawn) to self-destruct. Even with the time loss, mate can still be avoided by moving the e-pawn (9. . . . e6). Avarice wins and Black loses.

Related Zap: 1. d4 d5 2. c4 dxc4 3. Nf3 Nf6 4. e3 g6 5. Bxc4 Bg4 6. Ne5 Bxd1 7. Bxf7 + + (Queen's Gambit Declined).

Related Zap: 1. e4 c6 2. d4 d5 3. e5 Bf5 4. Ne2 h6 5. Ng3 Bh7 6. c4 dxc4 7. Bxc4 Nd7 8. Qh5 g6 9. e6 gxh5 10. exf7 + + (Caro-Kann Defense).

CARO-KANN DEFENSE 81

Removing the Guard

1. e4	c6
2. Nc3	d5
3. Nf3	dxe4
4. Nxe4	Bf5
5. Ng3	Bg6
6. h4	h6
7. Ne5	Bh7
8. Qh5	g6
9. Qf3	Qd5?

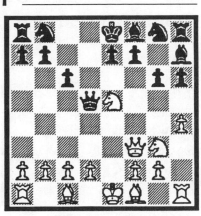

WHITE TO MOVE

Solution: The win is **10. Qxd5! cxd5 11. Bb5 +.** If 11. . . . Nc6, then 12. Nxc6 bxc6 13. Bxc6 + ; if 11. . . . Nd7, then 12. Bxd7 + ; and if 11. . . . Kd8, then 12. Nxf7 +.

Comment: Generally, you should exchange pieces, especially the queen, when you're under attack, so that there's less coming at you. But consider the consequences before making an actual trade. If it doesn't work, do something else.

Related Zap: 1. d4 d6 2. Nf3 Bg4 3. Nbd2 Bxf3 4. Nxf3 g6 5. e4 c5 6. dxc5 dxc5 7. Qxd8 + Kxd8 8. Ne5 Ke8 9. Bb5 + (Queen Pawn Game).

CARO-KANN DEFENSE **82**

Double Threat

1. e4	c6
2. d4	Na6
3. Bxa6	Qa5 +
4. Nc3	Qxa6
5. Qe2	b5
6. Nf3	d6
7. 0-0	

BLACK TO MOVE

Solution: Black gains the exchange with **7. . . . b4!**, when the knight can't safely move without hanging the queen. If 8. Qxa6, then after 8. . . . Bxa6, the knight is still attacked and so is the rook.

Comment: White thinks he's giving Black doubled pawns (3. Bxa6), but actually is surrendering bishop for knight and enabling Black's queen to assume a beautiful diagonal 4. . . . Qxa6). Moreover, 7. 0-0 turns out to be a losing move. Castle when the move is called for, not just because the possibility exists.

Mating Net

1. e4	c6
2. d4	d6
3. Nf3	Bg4
4. Nc3	Nd7
5. Bc4	e5
6. dxe5	Nxe5
7. Nxe5	Bxd1
8. Bxf7+	Ke7
9. Bxg8	Qa5?

WHITE TO MOVE

Solution: It's a three-piece mate: **10. Bg5+ Ke8 11. Bf7++**.

Comment: Black tries to save his queen (9. . . . Qa5?) and gets mated. If 9. . . . dxe5 instead, then White regains the queen (10. Bg5+) and stays at least a pawn ahead.

Related Zap: 1. e4 e5 2. Nf3 Nf6 3. Nxe5 Nc6 4. Nxc6 dxc6 5. d3 Bc5 6. Bg5 Nxe4 7. Bxd8 Bxf2+ 8. Ke2 Bg4++ (Petrov Defense).

CARO-KANN DEFENSE **84**

Mating Net

1.	e4	c6
2.	d4	d5
3.	Bd3	Nf6
4.	e5	Nfd7
5.	e6	fxe6?

WHITE TO MOVE

Solution: It's mate after **6. Qh5+ g6,** when White does it by **7. Bxg6+ hxg6 8. Qxg6++** or **7. Qxg6+ hxg6 8. Bxg6++**.

Comment: Black's third move is a mistake. Correct is to capture the e-pawn and then develop the king's knight. In the Caro-Kann, once White's bishop reaches d3, Black must be alert to advances and sacrifices that deflect the f-pawn because that opens the e8-h5 diagonal to a queen check at h5.

Related to Zap: 1. e4 b6 2. d4 Bb7 3. Bd3 f5 4. exf5 Bxg2 5. Qh5+ g6 6. fxg6 Nf6 7. gxh7+ Nxh5 8. Bg6++ (Owen Defense).

Related Zap: 1. d4 d5 2. c4 e6 3. Nc3 c6 4. Nf3 f6 5. Qc2 Ne7 6. e4 Nd7 7. Bd3 b6 8. 0-0 Bb7 9. Re1 a6 10. exd5 exd5 11. Bg6+ hxg6 12. Qxg6++ (Queen's Gambit Declined).

Discovery

1. e4	c6
2. d4	d5
3. Bd3	e6
4. Nf3	dxe4
5. Bxe4	Nf6
6. Bd3	Be7
7. Ne5	Qxd4
8. Nxf7!	Kxf7?

WHITE TO MOVE

Solution: The queen is gone: **9. Bg6 +! hxg6 10. Qxd4.**

Comment: If your opponent apparently lets a pawn hang, don't just take it. Before moving, try to find out if it's an oversight or a devious trap. Otherwise, you may not learn the truth until after the game, when you've lost.

Related Zap: 1. d4 d5 2. c4 dxc4 3. Nf3 Bg4 4. e3 e6 5. Bxc4 Nf6 6. Nc3 Nc6 7. 0-0 Bd6 8. Be2 0-0 9. e4 Bxf3 10. Bxf3 Nxd4 11. Qxd4 Bxh2 + 12. Kxh2 Qxd4 (Queen's Gambit Accepted).

CARO-KANN DEFENSE **86**

Discovery

1. e4	c6
2. d4	d5
3. Bd3	dxe4
4. Bxe4	c5
5. Nf3	Nf6
6. Bd3	cxd4
7. Nxd4	Qxd4?

WHITE TO MOVE

Solution: A case of greed. White discovers an attack to the queen, **8. Bb5 +,** taking it next move.

Comment: If your opponent plays six moves without blundering a piece, then gives away a knight in the middle of the board, think twice before taking it. Maybe it's a blunder. Maybe not.

Related Zap: 1. e4 e5 2. Nf3 d6 3. d4 Nd7 4. Bc4 Nb6 5. Bb3 exd4 6. Qxd4 Qf6 7. Qd3 Bg4 8. Bg5 Qxb2 9.Qb5 + c6 10. Bxf7 + Kxf7 11. Qxb2 (Philidor Defense).

CARO-KANN DEFENSE 87

Mating Net

1. e4	c6
2. d4	d5
3. e5	f6
4. Bd3	Nd7?

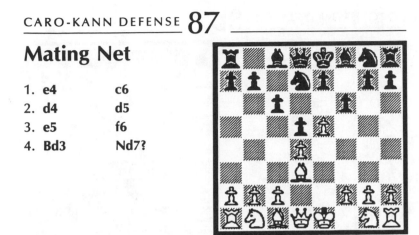

WHITE TO MOVE

Solution: Here's one mate: **5. Qh5+ g6 6. Bxg6+ hxg6 7. Qxg6++.** Here's two mate: 6. Qxg6+ hxg6+ 7. Bxg6++.

Comment: Once the f-pawn moves, Black must be concerned with the weakness along the e8-h5 diagonal. The problem is exacerbated when the white queen and bishop converge on the square g6. Throw in an obstructing knight at d7 and Black's a goner.

Related Zap: 1. e4 c6 2. d4 d5 3. e5 Bf5 4. Ne2 h6 5. Ng3 Bh7 6. c3 Nd7 7. e6 fxe6 8. Qh5+ g6 9. Be2 gxh5 10. Bxh5+ Bg6 11. Bxg6++ (Caro-Kann Defense).

88

Discovery

1. e4	c6
2. d4	d5
3. e5	e6
4. Bd3	c5
5. c3	Qb6
6. f4	cxd4
7. cxd4	Qxd4?

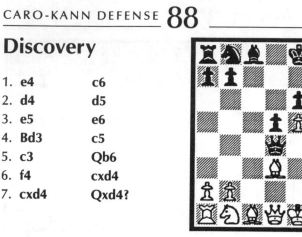

WHITE TO MOVE

Solution: Black's queen is dead as plastic after **8. Bb5+** and **9. Qxd4.**

Comment: It's usually unwise to go pawn-grabbing with the queen, especially early in the game. You lose time even when you get away with it, and Black doesn't get away with it.

Related Zap: 1. d4 Nf6 2. c4 g6 3. Nc3 d5 4. cxd5 Nxd5 5. e4 Nxc3 6. bxc3 Bg7 7. Bd3 c5 8. Ne2 cxd4 9. cxd4 Bxd4 10. Nxd4 Qxd4 11. Bb5+ (Gruenfeld Defense).

CARO-KANN DEFENSE 89

Trapping

1. e4	c6
2. d4	d5
3. e5	Bf5
4. h4	e6?

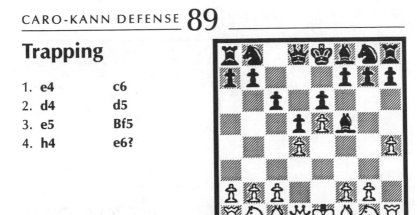

WHITE TO MOVE

Solution: The bishop is trapped after **5. g4!**, when **5. . . . Be4 6. f3 Bg6 7. h5** completes the snare.

Comment: Black's fourth move, denying the bishop escape, is a blunder. The piece can be saved on move four by playing the h-pawn to h6 or h5. A horde of mobile pawns can mean trouble for a bishop.

Related Zap: 1. g3 g6 2. Bg2 h5 3. Kf1 h4 4. Nf3 h3 (Benko Opening).

CARO-KANN DEFENSE **90**

Trapping

1. e4	c6
2. d4	d5
3. e5	Bf5
4. c4	Bxb1
5. Rxb1	Qa5 +
6. Bd2	Qxa2
7. Bc3	e6?

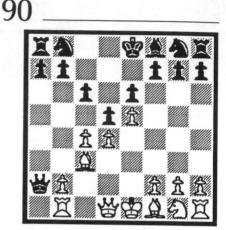

WHITE TO MOVE

Solution: Black snores and misses the snare: **8. Ra1.**

Comment: Generally, it's unwise to develop a piece and immediately exchange it for an undeveloped one, as Black does on the third and fourth moves. Black then compounds the problem by pawn-grabbing with the queen. This is not grand strategy.

Related Zap: 1. d4 d5 2. c4 c6 3. e3 Bf5 4. c5 Bxb1 5. Rxb1 Qa5 + 6. Bd2 Qxa2 7. Bc3 and then 8. Ra1 (Queen's Gambit Declined).

Trapping

1. e4	c6
2. d4	d5
3. e5	Bf5
4. Bd3	Bxd3
5. Qxd3	e6
6. Ne2	c5
7. c3	Ne7
8. Qb5+	Qd7
9 Qxc5?	

BLACK TO MOVE

Solution: There's no excuse for the queen after **9. ... Nf5 10. Qa5 b6.**

Comment: Even when the center is blocked, making a sudden counterstrike against your king less likely, be wary about pawn-grabbing with the queen. Otherwise, you become the fish you're trying to catch.

CARO-KANN DEFENSE 92

Mating Net

1. e4	c6
2. d4	d5
3. e5	Bf5
4. g4	Bg6
5. e6	fxe6
6. Nf3	Nd7
7. h4	h5
8. Bd3	Bxd3
9. Qxd3	hxg4?

WHITE TO MOVE

Solution: The game comes to a timely end with **10. Qg6 + +**.

Comment: Oversights are often made when you don't analyze your opponent's last move because it was simply a response to your previous move. It doesn't occur to you that it might also contain a threat. Black doesn't think twice about 9. Qxd3 because it's a recapture. So he gets mated.

Related Zap: 1. d4 f5 2. Bg5 h6 3. Bh4 g5 4. Bg3 f4 5. e3 h5 6. Bd3 Rh6 7. Qxh5 + Rxh5 8. Bg6 + + (Dutch Defense).

93

Discovery

1. e4	c6
2. d4	d5
3. exd5	cxd5
4. Bd3	Nf6
5. Bf4	Qb6
6. Nc3	e6
7. Nb5	Nc6
8. Bc7	Qa6

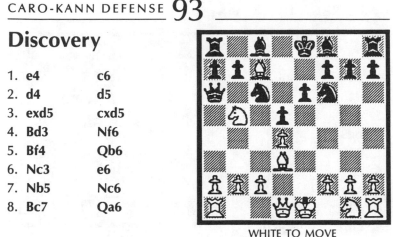

WHITE TO MOVE

Solution: White wins the queen for two pieces with **9. Nd6 + Bxd6 10. Bxa6.**

Comment: White also wins with 8. Nc7 + . Black should guard c7 with 7. . . . Na6. Although at a6 the knight doesn't attack the center, it meets the threat, and that's better than blindly following the maxim: a knight on the rim is dim. Generally, maxims sound good, but good moves win.

Related Zap: 1. d4 d5 2. c4 e6 3. Nc3 Nf6 4. cxd5 exd5 5. Bf4 Be7 6. e3 c6 7. Qc2 Nbd7 8. 0-0-0 Nh5 9. Nxd5 cxd5 10. Bc7 (Queen's Gambit Declined).

CARO-KANN DEFENSE 94

Double Threat

1. e4	c6
2. d4	d5
3. exd5	cxd5
4. Bd3	Nf6
5. Bf4	Nc6
6. c3	Bg4
7. Nf3	e6
8. Nbd2	Be7
9. Qb3	Qd7?
10. Ne5	Nxe5?

WHITE TO MOVE

Solution: White wins a piece with **11. dxe5!**. If the knight moves to safety, White pins the queen with the bishop.

Comment: Black's ninth move is wrong. Put the queen on c8 instead of d7 and the problem is minimized. It also helps to exchange the g4-bishop for the f3-knight so the knight can't go to e5 and attack the bishop.

CARO-KANN DEFENSE 95

Fork

1.	e4	c6
2.	d4	d5
3.	exd5	cxd5
4.	c4	Nc6
5.	c5?	b6
6.	b4	Nxb4?

WHITE TO MOVE

Solution: White emulsifies the knight at b4 with a forking queen check, **Qa4 +**.

Comment: Black blunders away the knight. But this shouldn't justify White's play, which is too expansive, too early. White's 5. c5? should be assailed by an immediate attack in the center. After 5. . . . e5, the edifice is ready to topple.

Removing the Guard

1. e4	c6
2. d4	d5
3. exd5	cxd5
4. c4	Nc6
5. Nf3	Bg4
6. cxd5	Qxd5
7. Be2	Bxf3?
8. Bxf3	Qxd4?

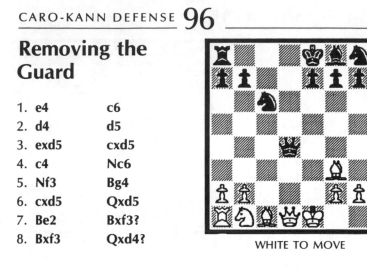

WHITE TO MOVE

Solution: White wins the queen by removing its defender, **9. Bxc6+.**

Comment: Black grabs a pawn and blunders away the queen. Instead of exchanging bishop for knight (7. . . . Bxf3), Black should continue development (7. . . . Nf6). Unless there's a mistake, unprepared attacks are easily repulsed.

Related Zap: 1. d4 d5 2. c4 dxc4 3. Nf3 Nc6 4. g3 Bg4 5. Bg2 Bxf3 6. Bxf3 Qxd4 7. Bxc6+ (Queen's Gambit Accepted)

CARO-KANN DEFENSE 97

Double Threat

1. e4	c6
2. d4	d5
3. exd5	cxd5
4. c4	Nf6
5. Nc3	Nc6
6. Nf3	g6
7. Bg5	Ne4
8. Nxd5?	Nxg5
9. Nxg5	

BLACK TO MOVE

Solution: White must lose a knight after 9. ... e6!.

Comment: The crime is pawn-grabbing (8. Nxd5?). The punishment is loss of a knight by double attack. On move eight, White should simply move the bishop to a safer square, say to e3 or h4.

Related Zap: 1. d4 Nf6 2. c4 g6 3. Nc3 d5 4. Nf3 Bg7 5. Bg5 Ne4 6. Nxd5 Nxg5 7. Nxg5 e6 (Gruenfeld Defense).

98

Trapping

1. e4	c6
2. d4	d5
3. exd5	cxd5
4. c4	Nf6
5. Nc3	Nc6
6. Nf3	Bg4
7. Be2	e6
8. 0-0	Be7
9. Be3	Qb6
10. a3	Qxb2?

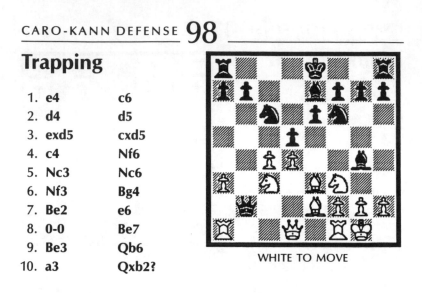

WHITE TO MOVE

Solution: The queen is trapped with **11. Na4.**

Comment: Black's ninth move attacks b2, but White's tenth move doesn't seem to defend it. Black should invest a couple of minutes to see if a clever trap is being set. Take time to prevent a blunder.

CARO-KANN DEFENSE **99**

Mating Net

1. e4	c6
2. d4	d5
3. Nc3	dxe4
4. Nxe4	Bf5
5. Qf3	e6
6. Be3	Nbd7
7. c3	Ngf6
8. Nd2	Be7
9. 0-0-0	Qa5
10. Bc4?	

BLACK TO MOVE

Solution: It's mate: 10. . . . Qxc3 ! ! 11. bxc3 Ba3 + +.

Comment: The final pattern given by the two bishops is called a criss-cross mate. It often happens when one player castles queenside and the opponent sacrifices the queen to lure away the b-pawn.

Related Zap: 1. e4 c6 2. d4 d5 3. Nc3 e6 4. Nf3 Bd7 5. Bf4 Na6 6. Qd3 Qe7 7. 0-0-0 0-0-0 8. Qxa6 bxa6 9. Bxa6 + + (Caro-Kann Defense).

CARO-KANN DEFENSE 100

Mating Net

1. e4	c6
2. d4	d5
3. Nc3	dxe4
4. Nxe4	Nf6
5. Qd3	e5
6. dxe5	Qa5+
7. Bd2	Qxe5
8. 0-0-0	Nxe4?

WHITE TO MOVE

Solution: It's mate in three: **9. Qd8+!! Kxd8 10. Bg5+**, and either **10. . . . Kc7 11. Bd8++** or **10. . . . Ke8 11. Rd8++**.

Comment: The only way to get out of double check is to move the king. When a double check is executed properly, neither of the checking units can be captured and miracles occur.

Related Zap: 1. e4 c5 2. d4 cxd4 3. Qxd4 Qa5+ 4. Bd2 Qh5 5. Nf3 d6 6. Na3 Nc6 7. Bb5 Nf6 8. 0-0-0 g6 9. e5 dxe5 10. Qd8+ Kxd8 11. Ba5+ Ke8 12. Rd8++ (Sicilian Defense).

Related Zap: 1. e4 c5 2. Nf3 d6 3. d4 cxd4 4. Qxd4 Nc6 5. Bb5 Nf6 6. Bg5 h6 7. Bd2 g6 8. 0-0 Bg7 9. Rd1 Nh5 10. e5 dxe5 11. Qxd8+ Kxd8 12. Ba5+ Ke8 13. Rd8++ (Sicilian Defense).

CARO-KANN DEFENSE 101

Fork

1. e4	c6
2. d4	d5
3. Nc3	dxe4
4. Nxe4	Nf6
5. Ng3	h5
6. h4	Qc7
7. Be2	Bg4
8. Bxg4	Nxg4
9. Nxh5?	

BLACK TO MOVE

Solution: Black wins the knight with **9. . . . Qa5 +!**. Next move, Black's queen takes on h5 and also defends g4.

Comment: In sacrificing the knight on h5, White thinks Black must retake with the rook, abandoning the g4-knight to White's queen. But White overlooks the intervention of a forking queen check at a5. Before playing any tactical sequence, take one last look to make sure a surprise check doesn't upset the apple cart.

102

Double Threat

1. e4	c6
2. d4	d5
3. Nc3	dxe4
4. Nxe4	Nf6
5. Ng3	h5
6. Bg5	h4
7. Bxf6	hxg3
8. Be5	Rxh2
9. Rxh2	Qa5 +
10. c3	

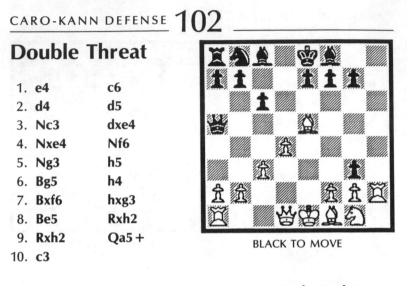

BLACK TO MOVE

Solution: Black scores with **10. . . . Qxe5 + ! 11. dxe5 gxh2,** soon making a new queen.

Comment: When a pawn on its seventh rank attacks a knight, it threatens to make a queen in two ways: by advancing or by taking the knight. This two-pronged threat often makes surprising combinations possible, such as 10. . . . Qxe5 + !.

Related Zap: 1. d4 d5 2. c4 c6 3. Nf3 Bf5 4. Qb3 Qb6 5. cxd5 Qxb3 6. axb3 Bxb1 7. dxc6 Be4 8. Rxa7 Rxa7 9. c7 (Queen's Gambit Declined).

CARO-KANN DEFENSE 103

Fork

1. e4	c6
2. d4	d5
3. Nc3	dxe4
4. Nxe4	Nf6
5. Nxf6+	exf6
6. Bc4	Qe7+
7. Ne2?	

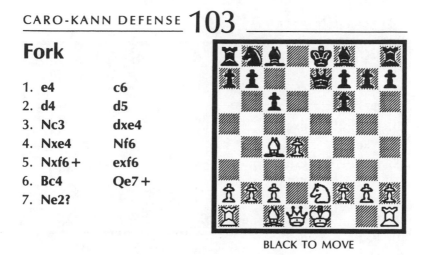

BLACK TO MOVE

Solution: White's hands are tied by 7. . . . **Qb4+**, forking king and bishop. The bishop goes.

Comment: White can avoid losing the piece by answering the check with the queen, 7. Qe2. In that case, White would have a healthier pawn structure. Many players irrationally avoid a queen trade, even when it's desirable. Trade queens if it gives any advantage, no matter how small.

104

Fork

1. **e4**	**c6**
2. **d4**	**d5**
3. **Nc3**	**dxe4**
4. **Nxe4**	**Nf6**
5. **Nxf6 +**	**gxf6**
6. **Ne2**	**Bf5**
7. **Ng3**	**Bg6**
8. **h4**	**h5**
9. **Be2**	**Nd7**
10. **Nxh5**	**Bxh5**
11. **Bxh5**	

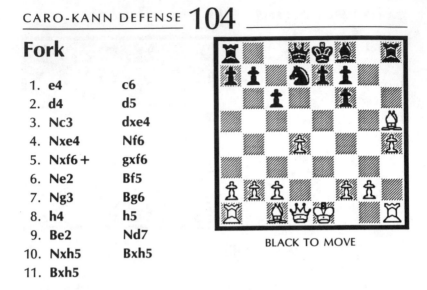

BLACK TO MOVE

Solution: Black wins the bishop with **11. . . . Qa5 +**.

Comment: Generally, a queen check at a5 can offer several different forking possibilities (along the a-file, the fifth rank, and the a5-e1 diagonal). This is a slightly unusual way to exploit the fifth rank.

Mating Net

1. e4   c6
2. d4   d5
3. Nc3   dxe4
4. Nxe4   Nbd7
5. Qe2   Ngf6?

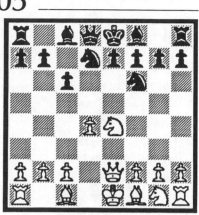

WHITE TO MOVE

Solution: It's a one-mover, **6. Nd6+ +!**, smothered mate. Black's e-pawn is pinned and can't capture the knight.

Comment: Black's fourth move prepares his fifth move, which is played automatically, without analyzing White's unusual queen development. When your opponent begins reasonably but suddenly plays strangely, examine the position with particular care. Maybe a trap is being set.

Related Zap: 1. d4 Nf6 2. c4 e5 3. dxe5 Ng4 4. Bf4 Bb4+ 5. Nd2 Nc6 6. Nf3 Qe7 7. a3 Ngxe5 8. axb4 Nd3+ + (Budapest Defense).

CARO-KANN DEFENSE 106

Unpin

1. **e4**	**c6**
2. **d4**	**d5**
3. **Nc3**	**dxe4**
4. **Nxe4**	**Nd7**
5. **Nf3**	**Ngf6**
6. **Nxf6 +**	**Nxf6**
7. **Bc4**	**Bg4?**

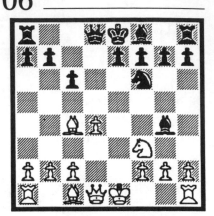

WHITE TO MOVE

Solution: White pilfers a pawn with **8. Bxf7 +! Kxf7 9. Ne5 + Ke8 10. Nxg4.**

Comment: It's simple. Black shouldn't pin the f3-knight if White can sacrifice on f7 and give a follow-up knight check on e5. It just loses a pawn.

Related Zap: 1. d4 d5 2. c4 c6 3. Nf3 Bg4 4. e3 dxc4 5. Bxc4 b5 6. Bxf7 + Kxf7 7. Ne5 + (Queen's Gambit Declined).

CARO-KANN DEFENSE 107

Fork

1. e4	c6
2. d4	d5
3. Nc3	dxe4
4. Nxe4	Nd7
5. Nf3	Ngf6
6. Nxf6+	Nxf6
7. Ne5	Bf5
8. c3	g6

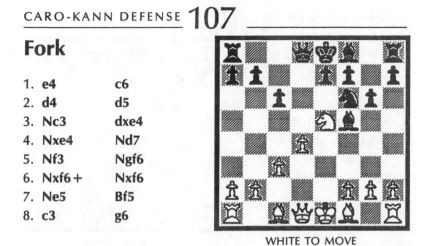

WHITE TO MOVE

Solution: White cashes in with **9. Qb3!,** assailing b7 and f7.

Comment: When White has a knight on e5 (or an unimpeded bishop on c4), the square f7 is under direct attack. If Black develops the queen bishop early, it leaves b7 undefended. A standard tactic is to play the White queen to b3, hitting f7 and b7. Black can't defend both targets simultaneously.

CARO-KANN DEFENSE **108**

Mating Net

1. e4	c6
2. d4	d5
3. Nc3	dxe4
4. Nxe4	Nd7
5. Ng5	h6
6. Ne6	fxe6?

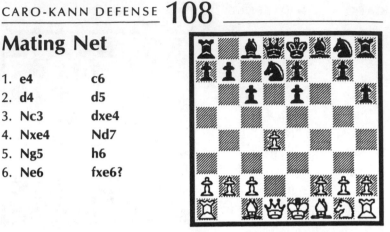

WHITE TO MOVE

Solution: Black's last move self-mates: **7. Qh5+ g6 8. Qxg6++**.

Comment: Instead of taking the knight (6. . . . fxe6?), Black should move the queen to b6 or a5. The sacrifice of a knight on e6 becomes more likely if a Black knight obstructs d7 and the rook pawn has moved to h6.

Related Zap: 1. d4 Nf6 2. Nd2 e5 3. dxe5 Ng4 4. h3 Ne3 5. fxe3 Qh4+ 6. g3 Qxg3++ (Queen Pawn Game).

Pin

1. e4	c6
2. d4	d5
3. Nc3	dxe4
4. Nxe4	Nd7
5. Ng5	h6
6. Ne6	Qa5 +
7. Bd2	Qb6
8. Bd3	fxe6?
9. Qh5 +	Kd8

WHITE TO MOVE

Solution: Black's queen is mashed potatoes after **10. Ba5!**. Pin and win.

Comment: Black thinks the knight can be taken because the king has an apparent escape square at d8, overlooking that White's bishop can move to a5, supported by the queen from across the board. Black gets it on both flanks.

Related Zap: 1. d4 d5 2. c4 c6 3. Nf3 Nf6 4. e3 g6 5. Nc3 Bg7 6. Qb3 0-0 7. Bd2 Qb6 8. Qa3 e6 9. cxd5 exd5 10. Na4 Qd8 11. Nb6 Qxb6 12. Ba5 (Queen's Gambit Declined).

Mating Attack

1. **e4**	**c6**
2. **d4**	**d5**
3. **Nc3**	**dxe4**
4. **Nxe4**	**Nd7**
5. **Bc4**	**Ngf6**
6. **Ng5**	**e6**
7. **Qe2**	**h6**

WHITE TO MOVE

Solution: This main winning line is **8. Nxf7! Kxf7 9. Qxe6+ Kg6 10. Bd3+ Kh5 11. Qh3++.**

Comment: Black's attempt to drive away the knight fails. Instead of retreating, the knight is given up for attack. Before playing a weakening pawn move, such as 7. . . . h6?, make sure you see that it actually achieves its aim.

Related Zap: 1. d4 d5 2. c4 dxc4 3. Nf3 Nf6 4. e3 e6 5. Bxc4 c5 6. Qe2 cxd4 7. exd4 Nbd7 8. Ne5 Be7 9. Nxf7 Kxf7 10. Qxe6+ Kg6 11. Bd3+ Kh5 12. Qh3++ (Queen's Gambit Accepted).

Direct Attack

1. e4	c6
2. d4	d5
3. Nc3	dxe4
4. Nxe4	Nd7
5. Bc4	Ngf6
6. Ng5	e6
7. Qe2	Nb6
8. Bd3	Qxd4?
9. N1f3	Qd8

WHITE TO MOVE

Solution: White scores with **10. Nfe5!**, and f7 can't be defended.

Comment: It's a case of pawn-grabbing. Instead of taking the d-pawn (8. . . . Qxd4?), Black should attack the g5-knight. Don't allow an enemy piece to perch unencumbered in your half of the board. If you have the time, and the situation allows, drive it away.

4

MODERN DEFENSE

(TRAPS 112-121)

1. e4 g6

TRAPS	WHITE'S 2ND MOVE	BLACK'S 2ND MOVE
112-117	2. d4	2. . . . Bg7
118-121	2. d4	2. . . . d6

PIRC DEFENSE

(TRAPS 122-137)

1. e4 d6 2. d4 Nf6

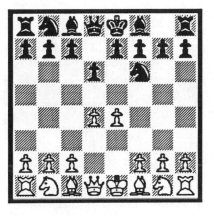

TRAPS	WHITE'S 3RD MOVE	BLACK'S 3RD MOVE
122	3. e5	3. . . . Ne4
123	3. Qf3	3. . . . b6
124	3. Nc3	3. . . . c5
125-137	3. Nc3	3. . . . g6

MODERN DEFENSE **112**

Fork

1. e4	g6
2. d4	Bg7
3. Be3	d6
4. Qd2	Nf6
5. f3	e5
6. d5	Nfd7
7. Bh6?	

BLACK TO MOVE

Solution: Black gains the intrusive bishop with **7. . . . Qh4+!.**

Comment: When Black retreats his knight from f6 to d7 without provocation, White should assume there's a reason until analysis proves otherwise. Anyone can be snared by not thinking.

Related Zap: 1. d4 Nf6 2. c4 g6 3. Nc3 Bg7 4. e4 d6 5. f3 0-0 6. Be3 e5 7. d5 Ne8 8. Qd2 f5 9. Bh6 Qh4+ (King's Indian Defense).

Related Zap: 1. Nf3 Nc6 2. g3 e5 3. d3 d5 4. Nbd2 f6 5. Bg2 Be6 6. e4 dxe4 7. dxe4 Qd7 8. 0-0 Bh3 9. Nxe5 fxe5 10. Qh5+ (King's Indian Attack).

113

Removing the Guard

1. e4	g6
2. d4	Bg7
3. Nf3	d6
4. c4	Nd7
5. Ng5	Nh6

WHITE TO MOVE

Solution: White triumphs by **6. Bxf7 + !**. No matter how Black answers, the knight jumps to e6 and wins the queen.

Comment: The real culprit is the knight at d7. It blocks out the c8-bishop, destroying Black's ability to fight for e6.

Related Zap: 1. e4 e5 2. Nf3 d6 3. Bc4 Nd7 4. d3 a6 5. Ng5 Nh6 6. 0-0 Be7 7. Bxf7 + Nxf7 8. Ne6 (Philidor Defense).

Related Zap: 1. d4 e6 2. Bf4 Ne7 3. Nc3 b6 4. Nb5 Na6 5. Bxc7 Nxc7 6. Nd6 + + (Queen Pawn Game).

MODERN DEFENSE **114**

Mating Net

1. e4	g6
2. d4	Bg7
3. Nf3	d6
4. Bc4	Nd7?
5. Bxf7+!	Kxf7
6. Ng5+	Kf6

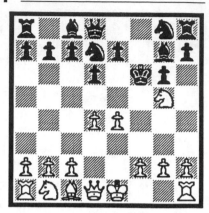

WHITE TO MOVE

Solution: It's mate on the move: **7. Qf3++**.

Comment: White's fifth-move sacrifice works because Black has lost control of e6 after developing the knight to d7. After 5. Bxf7+, Black's best defense is to refuse the bishop, moving his king to f8. Black would be losing but still alive.

Related Zap: 1. g3 e5 2. Bg2 Nf6 3. d3 Bc5 4. Nd2 Bxf2+ 5. Kxf2 Ng4+ 6. Kf3 Qf6+ 7. Kxg4 d6+ 8. Kh5 Qh6++ (Benko Opening).

MODERN DEFENSE 115

Trapping

1. e4   g6
2. d4   Bg7
3. Nc3   Nf6
4. e5   Nh5?

WHITE TO MOVE

Solution: White wins the knight with **5. g4.**

Comment: A knight on the rim is dim aphoristically, esthetically, practically, strategically, and, in this case, tactically. Don't put it there without a good reason.

Related Zap: 1. e4 e5 2. Nf3 Nc6 3. d4 exd4 4. c3 Nf6 5. e5 Nh5 6. g4 (Scotch Gambit).

MODERN DEFENSE 116

Overload

1. e4	g6
2. d4	Bg7
3. Nc3	d6
4. Bc4	c6
5. Nf3	b5?

WHITE TO MOVE

Solution: White's surprise combination, **6. Nxb5! cxb5 7. Bd5,** gains the exchange.

Comment: Black begins his queenside operations too soon. White's shot (6. Nxb5!) doesn't work if Black first develops the king knight to f6 or his queen knight to d7 or a6 before playing the pawn to b5. A little preparation is called for.

Related Zap: 1. d4 d5 2. c4 c6 3. Nc3 dxc4 4. e4 e5 5. Bxc4 exd4 6. Nf3 b5 7. Nxb5 cxb5 8. Bd5 (Queen's Gambit Declined).

Mating Net

1. e4	g6
2. d4	Bg7
3. Nc3	d6
4. g3	Nc6
5. d5	Nd4
6. Ng2?	

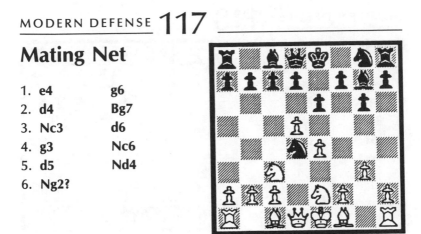

BLACK TO MOVE

Solution: Black's smothered mate, **6. . . . Nf3+ +**, is most convincing.

Comment: By developing the queen bishop to e3, or the king bishop to g2, White's game is perfectly fine. Generally, it's counterproductive to begin a fianchetto development and delay completing it. White's bishop never gets to g2.

Related Zap: 1. e4 e5 2. Nf3 Nc6 3. Bb5 d6 4. Nc3 g6 5. d4 exd4 6. Nd5 Nge7 7. Nf6+ + (Ruy Lopez).

Related Zap: 1. g4 Nc6 2. e4 Nd4 3. Ne2 Nf3+ + (Grob's Attack).

MODERN DEFENSE **118**

Fork

1. e4   g6
2. d4   d6
3. Bc4   Nf6
4. e5?   dxe5
5. dxe5

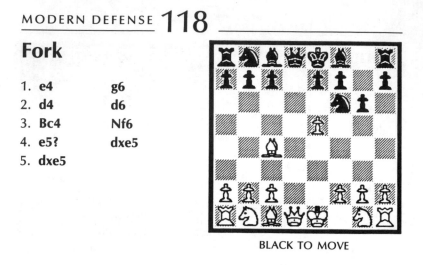

BLACK TO MOVE

Solution: Black wins a pawn with **5. . . . Qxd1+ 6. Kxd1 Ng4.**

Comment: Many players are reluctant to trade queens early in the game, even when it wins a pawn. They say something like, "I need my queen." Does this mean the other side doesn't? If you think like this, you probably wouldn't know what to do with your queen anyway.

Related Zap: 1. e4 e5 2. Nf3 d6 3. d4 Bg4 4. dxe5 dxe5 5. Qxd8+ Kxd8 6. Nxe5 (Philidor Defense).

Unpin

1. e4	g6
2. d4	d6
3. Nf3	Bg4
4. Bc4	Nd7?

WHITE TO MOVE

Solution: White comes out a pawn ahead after **5. Bxf7 + ! Kxf7 6. Ng5 + Ke8 7. Qxg4.**

Comment: White's fourth move threatens the sacrifice on f7, so Black's fourth move makes no sense. It's not right; it's not even wrong. Respond to your opponent. Don't play automatically and your play automatically improves.

Related Zap: 1. d4 e6 2. d5 Nf6 3. Bg5 Bc5 4. Nc3 Bxf2 + 5. Kxf2 Ng4 + 6. Ke1 Qxg5 (Queen's Gambit Declined).

MODERN DEFENSE 120

Unpin

1. e4	g6
2. d4	d6
3. Nf3	Bg4
4. Nc3	Nc6
5. d5	Ne5?

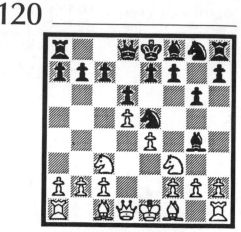

WHITE TO MOVE

Solution: After **6. Nxe5! Bxd1 7. Bb5 + c6 8. dxc6,** White is going to regain the queen with interest. For example, 8. . . . Qc7 9. cxb7 + Kd8 10. Nxf7 + + ; or 8. . . . Qb6 9. cxb7 + Kd8 10. bxa8(Q) + .

Comment: Breaking the pin by capturing on e5 and following with a bishop check on b5 is a familiar theme. It works when Black doesn't have a satisfactory way to meet the bishop check.

MODERN DEFENSE 121

Unpin

1. e4	g6
2. d4	d6
3. Nf3	Bg4
4. Nc3	Nc6
5. Bc4	e5
6. dxe5	Nxe5?

WHITE TO MOVE

Solution: White wins a piece by **7. Nxe5!**. If Black takes the queen, it's mate: 7. . . . Bxd1 8. Bxf7+ Ke7 9. Nd5++.

Comment: Black can avoid all this by playing 6. . . . dxe5 instead of taking on e5 with the knight. At least that doesn't lose a piece.

Related Zap: 1. e4 e5 2. Nf3 Nc6 3. Bc4 h6 4. Nc3 d6 5. d4 Bg4 6. dxe5 Nxe5 7. Nxe5 Bxd1 8. Bxf7+ Ke7 9. Nd5++ (Three Knights Game).

PIRC DEFENSE 122

Trapping

1. e4   d6
2. d4   Nf6
3. e5   Ne4?

WHITE TO MOVE

Solution: The knight is engulfed, **4. f3,** and Black doesn't quite get enough compensation for it.

Comment: When a knight goes behind enemy lines without support and without retreat, what happens when it's attacked? Don't use the ingress when there's no egress.

Related Zap: 1. d4 f5 2. c4 Nc6 3. Nc3 e5 4. d5 Nd4 5. e3 (Dutch Defense).

123

Discovery

1. e4   d6
2. d4   Nf6
3. Qf3   b6?

WHITE TO MOVE

Solution: With **4. e5,** White attacks the knight and the rook in the corner. Black may save the one of his choosing.

Comment: Instead of the blunder 3. . . . b6?, Black can take aim at d4, weakened by the queen's departure. The queen pawn can be attacked by either Nb8-c6, c7-c5, or c7-e5. Another good move is 3. . . . g6.

Related Zap: 1. e4 e5 2. f4 exf4 3. Bc4 Qh4+ 4. Kf1 b5 5. Bxb5 Nf6 6. Qf3 g5 7. e5 Ng4 8. g3 (King's Gambit Accepted).

Interference

1.	e4	d6
2.	d4	Nf6
3.	Nc3	c5
4.	dxc5	Qa5
5.	cxd6	Nxe4?
6.	Qd5	Nc5

WHITE TO MOVE

Solution: A divisive bishop check, **7. Bb5 + !,** separates Black's queen and knight and wins a piece. If 7. . . . Bd7, then 8. Qxc5 puts the knight back in the box.

Comment: Using the queen to pin the queen knight, followed by capturing the enemy king pawn, is common. One factor mitigating against it is time. Here, the Black knight makes three moves to free itself, and White uses the extra tempi to make a point.

Discovery

1. e4	d6
2. d4	Nf6
3. Nf3	g6
4. Bc4	Bg7
5. Qe2	0-0
6. e5	Nfd7
7. e6	fxe6
8. Qxe6+	Kh8
9. Ng5?	

BLACK TO MOVE

Solution: The queen is harrassed by **9. . . . Ne5!.** If 10. Qd5, then 10. . . . c6 wins the c4-bishop.

Comment: White evinces a faulty plan from moves five to nine, moving both the e-pawn and queen twice to set up an empty threat to Black's king, then trying to exploit an apparently weakened f7 with 9. Ng5. But the attack is premature.

Related Zap: 1. e4 c5 2. Nf3 Nc6 3. d4 cxd4 4. Nxd4 e6 5. Nc3 a6 6. g3 Nge7 7. Nb3 d6 8. Bg2 Bd7 9. Qxd6 Nd5 (Sicilian Defense).

PIRC DEFENSE 126

Removing the Guard

1. e4	d6
2. d4	Nf6
3. Nc3	g6
4. Bg5	e5
5. dxe5	dxe5?

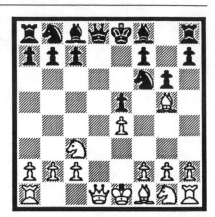

WHITE TO MOVE

Solution: Black loses the house: **6. Qxd8+ Kxd8 7. Bxf6+.**

Comment: If you begin the flanking of your king's bishop by moving the knight-pawn, please complete the fianchetto by moving the bishop to knight two. Don't break the sequence without a sound reason. Once you've moved the g-pawn, try to avoid moving the e-pawn, especially if it jeopardizes your king knight.

Related Zap: 1. d4 Nf6 2. c4 g6 3. Nc3 d6 4. Nf3 Nbd7 5. Bg5 e5 6. dxe5 dxe5 7. Nxe5 Nxe5 8. Qxd8+ Kxd8 9. Bxf6+ (King's Indian Defense).

Overload

1. e4	d6
2. d4	Nf6
3. Nc3	g6
4. Bg5	Nbd7
5. f4	h6
6. Bh4	Nh5
7. Nge2	Nxf4?
8. Nxf4	g5

WHITE TO MOVE

Solution: White wins the queen with **9. Ne6!**, for 9. . . . fxe6 allows 10. Qh5 mate.

Comment: Black's pawn trick fails for two reasons: because of the weaknesses along the e8-h5 diagonal; and because the d7-knight blocks the c8-bishop's control of e6.

Related Zap: 1. d4 d5 2. Nf3 Nf6 3. Bg5 Nbd7 4. e3 Ne4 5. Nbd2 Nxg5 6. Nxg5 h6 7. Ne6 fxe6 8. Qh5+ g6 9. Qxg6++ (Queen Pawn Game).

PIRC DEFENSE 128
Overload

1. e4   d6
2. d4   Nf6
3. Nc3   g6
4. Bg5   Bg7
5. f4   c5
6. e5   Ng4
7. Bb5 + Nc6?

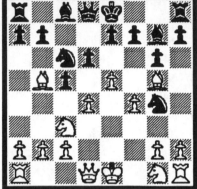

WHITE TO MOVE

Solution: White wins a piece with **8. d5 a6 9. dxc6 axb5 10. cxb7 Bxb7 11. Qxg4.**

Comment: Black cannot survive by blocking the check along the a4-e8 diagonal (7. . . . Bd7 is met by 8. Qxg4!), but has to move the king to f8. This forfeits the right to castle, but it's better than losing a piece.

Related Zap: 1. e4 c5 2. Nc3 d6 3. f4 g6 4. d4 Nf6 5. e5 Ng4 6. Bb5 + Nc6 7. d5 a6 8. dxc6 axb5 9. cxb7 Bxb7 10. Qxg4 (Sicilian Defense).

Pin

1.	e4	d6
2.	d4	Nf6
3.	Nc3	g6
4.	Bg5	Bg7
5.	f4	c5
6.	e5	cxd4?
7.	exf6	exf6

WHITE TO MOVE

Solution: White stays a piece ahead with **8. Qxd4!**, pinning the f6-pawn to the bishop at g7.

Comment: On move six, White pushes on Black's knight. Black should respond to this attack and avoid the loss of a piece. Inserting a counterthreat (6. . . . cxd4?) fails because White's attack comes first.

Related Zap: 1. d4 Nf6 2. c4 g6 3. Nc3 Bg7 4. e4 d6 5. Nf3 Nbd7 6. Bg5 c5 7. e5 cxd4 8. exf6 exf7 9. Qxd4 (King's Indian Defense).

PIRC DEFENSE **130**

Removing the Guard

1.	e4	d6
2.	d4	Nf6
3.	Nc3	g6
4.	Bg5	Bg7
5.	e5	dxe5
6.	dxe5	Qxd1+
7.	Rxd1	Ng4?
8	h3	Nxe5

WHITE TO MOVE

Solution: Black doesn't have a satisfactory reply to **9. Nd5!**, when 9. . . . Na6 10. Bxa6 leaves c7 indefensible. And if 9. . . . Kd8, then 10. Nb6+ wins.

Comment: Actually, Black does a little better by shifting the knight to d7 instead of g4. By moving the knight to g4 and being forced to use it to capture on e5, Black becomes unable to transfer the bishop to e5 to guard c7.

Related Zap: 1. e4 e5 2. Nc3 g6 3. d4 d6 4. dxe5 dxe5 5. Qxd8+ Kxd8 6. Bg5+ f6 7. 0-0-0+ Ke8 8. Nd5 (Vienna Game).

Removing the Guard

1. e4	d6
2. d4	Nf6
3. Nc3	g6
4. Nf3	Bg7
5. Bc4	c6
6. Be3?	b5
7. Bb3	

BLACK TO MOVE

Solution: The e-pawn falls after 7. . . . **b4.**

Comment: On the surface, Black's pawn attack has to do with flank play. But by forcing the c3-knight to move, Black really hits White's e-pawn. White could stop Black's planned b7-b5 (telegraphed by 5. . . . c6) with 6. a4.

Related Zap: 1. e4 e5 2. Nf3 d6 3. Bc4 Be7 4. d4 Nd7 5. Nc3 Ngf6 6. 0-0 0-0 7. h3 c6 8. Be3 b5 9. Bb3 b4 (Philidor Defense).

PIRC DEFENSE 132
Saving

1. e4	d6
2. d4	Nf6
3. Nc3	g6
4. Nf3	Bg7
5. Bc4	c5
6. Be3	Nxe4?
7. Nxe4	d5

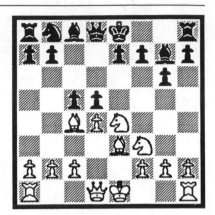

WHITE TO MOVE

Solution: White keeps the extra piece with **8. Bb5+ Bd7 9. Bxd7+**, followed by saving the knight on e4. If 8. . . . Kf8, then 9. Nc3 is sufficient.

Comment: In the fork trick, a knight is surrendered to break up the enemy pawn center. A pawn fork then regains the sacrificed piece. This stratagem fails, however, if one of the forked pieces can be saved with a gain of time.

Related Zap: 1. e4 e5 2. Nf3 Nc6 3. Bc4 Bc5 4. Nxe5 Nxe5 5. d4 Nxc4 (Giuoco Piano).

Double Threat

1. e4	d6
2. d4	Nf6
3. Nc3	g6
4. Nf3	Bg7
5. Be2	0-0
6. 0-0	Nbd7
7. e5	dxe5
8. dxe5	Ng4
9. e6!	fxe6?

WHITE TO MOVE

Solution: The invasion **10. Ng5!** attacks g4 and e6. Black must surrender the exchange.

Comment: Be careful about developing the queen knight to d7. Sometimes it works well, but on other occasions it deprives the f6-knight of a useful retreat.

Related Zap: 1. d4 Nf6 2. c4 g6 3. Nc3 Bg7 4. e4 d6 5. Nf3 0-0 6. Be2 Nbd7 7. 0-0 b6 8. e5 dxe5 9. dxe5 Ng4 10. e6 fxe6 11. Ng5 (King's Indian Defense).

PIRC DEFENSE 134

Pin

1.	e4	d6
2.	d4	Nf6
3.	Nc3	g6
4.	f4	c5
5.	e5	Ng4
6.	Bb5+	Bd7

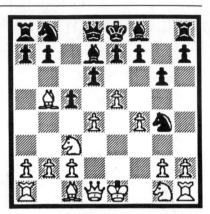

WHITE TO MOVE

Solution: The knight at g4 isn't really protected: **8. Qxg4!** wins it for free.

Comment: Black has an optical illusion. Because the knight at g4 is in line with the d7-bishop, Black assumes it's protected. But the bishop is pinned to its king and can't move off the a4-e8 diagonal.

135

Double Threat

1. e4	d6
2. d4	Nf6
3. Nc3	g6
4. f4	Bg7
5. Nf3	c5
6. Bb5 +	Bd7
7. e5	Bxb5?

WHITE TO MOVE

Solution: White wins a piece with **8. exf6,** after which both of Black's bishops are hanging.

Comment: Black fares better by moving f6-knight in response to White's pawn advance. Try not to lose your pieces. Lose your opponent's pieces.

PIRC DEFENSE **136**

Discovery

1. **e4**	**d6**
2. **d4**	**Nf6**
3. **Nc3**	**g6**
4. **f4**	**Bg7**
5. **Nf3**	**c5**
6. **dxc5**	**Qa5**
7. **Bb5 +**	**Bd7**
8. **Qe2?**	

BLACK TO MOVE

Solution: Black gets the upper hand with **8. . . . Nxe4!**. However White plays, the ensuing Bg7xc3 + and its ramifications spell trouble. The likely line leaves Black with an extra pawn: 9. Bxd7 + Nxd7 10. Qxe4 Bxc3 + 11. Bd2 Bxd2 + 12.Nxd2 Nxc5.

Comment: White should steer clear of 8. Qe2 and play 8. Bxd7 +, followed by 9. 0-0. The queen move keeps White's king in the center and gives Black the edge.

Discovery

1. e4	d6
2. d4	Nf6
3. Nc3	g6
4. f4	Bg7
5. Nf3	0-0
6. e5	dxe5
7. fxe5	Nd5
8. Bc4	Be6
9. 0-0?	

BLACK TO MOVE

Solution: Black wins a piece with **9. . . . Nxc3,** for 10. bxc3 is followed by 10. . . . Bxc4.

Comment: White can avoid losing a piece by delaying castling until bishops and knights have been exchanged on d5. Another way to save the bishop is to protect it, with either 9. Qe2 or 9. Bb3.

Related Zap: 1. e4 c6 2. d4 d5 3. Nc3 dxe4 4. Nxe4 Nf6 5. Qd3 Bf5 6. Nxf6 + exf6 7. Qxf5 (Caro-Kann Defense).

Related Zap: 1. d4 d5 2. c3 c6 3. Nd2 Nd7 4. e4 dxe4 5. Nxe4 Ndf6 6. Bd3 Bf5 7. Nxf6 + Nxf6 8. Bxf5 (Queen Pawn Game).

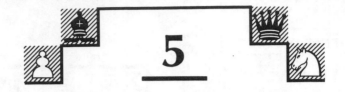

5

FRENCH DEFENSE

(TRAPS 138-182)

1. e4 e6

TRAPS	WHITE'S 2ND MOVE	BLACK'S 2ND MOVE
138	2. b3	2. . . . d5
139	2. Bc4	2. . . . d5
140	2. d3	2. . . . b6
141	2. d3	2. . . . d5
142	2. d4	2. . . . d5
143	2. Nf3	2. . . . d5
144	2. d4	2. . . . b6
145	2. d4	2. . . . Nf6
146-182	2. d4	2. . . . d5

TRAPS	WHITE'S 3RD MOVE	BLACK'S 3RD MOVE
146	3. f3	3. . . . dxe4
147-148	3. exd5	3. . . . exd5
149	3. Nd2	3. . . . Nc6
150-151	3. Nd2	3. . . . c5
152	3. e5	3. . . . f6
153-154	3. e5	3. . . . b6
155-159	3. e5	3. . . . c5
160	3. e5	3. . . . Nf6
161-169	3. Nc3	3. . . . Bb4
170-182	3. Nc3	3. . . . dxe4

FRENCH DEFENSE **138**

Fork

1. **e4**	**e6**
2. **b3**	**d5**
3. **Nc3**	**Nf6**
4. **Bd3?**	**dxe4**
5. **Nxe4?**	**Nxe4**
6. **Bxe4**	

BLACK TO MOVE

Solution: Black gives an embarrassing fork to rook and bishop, **6. . . . Qd4!**.

Comment: It's usually a bad idea to develop the king bishop in front of the d-pawn, preventing its movement. To get out the queen bishop in such instances, it becomes necessary to move the b-pawn. Sometimes the solution to one problem is a new problem.

Related Zap: 1. f4 Nf6 2. Nf3 d6 3. b3 e5 4. fxe5 dxe5 5. Nxe5 Qd4 (Bird's Opening).

FRENCH DEFENSE **139**

Trapping

1. e4   e6
2. Bc4?   d5
3. exd5   exd5
4. Bb5+   c6
5. Ba4   a5
6. Nf3?

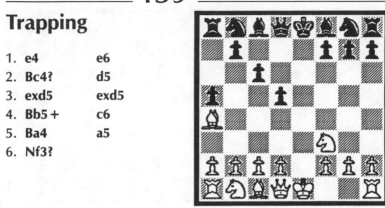

BLACK TO MOVE

Solution: Bye-bye bishop after **6. . . . b5 7. Bb3 a4.**

Comment: Don't develop the king bishop to c4 if Black can kick it in the teeth with the d-pawn. Don't use it to check at b5 if the c-pawn can be stuck in its face. And if Black threatens to surround it with pawns, give it an escape (6. c2-c3, for example).

Related Zap: 1. c4 e6 2. g3 Bb4 3. a3 Ba5 4. b4 Bb6 5. c5 (English Opening).

Related Zap: 1. e4 e5 2. d3 Bb4+ 3. c3 Ba5 4. a4 d6 5. b4 Bb6 6. a5 (King Pawn Game).

Related Zap: 1. d4 d5 2. f3 Bf5 3. Bf4 e6 4. e3 g6 5. g4 (Queen Pawn Game).

Unpin

1. **e4**	**e6**
2. **d3**	**b6**
3. **Nf3**	**Bb7**
4. **g3**	**d5**
5. **Nbd2**	**Bb4**
6. **Bg2**	**dxe4**
7. **dxe4**	**Bxe4?**

WHITE TO MOVE

Solution: After **8. c3!**, the d2-knight is free to take the on e4. (On 8. . . . Bxf3 9. Qxf3, two Black pieces are hanging.)

Comment: Don't put your faith in a pin that can be broken with a gain of time. Otherwise, you might suddenly find yourself facing two simultaneous threats: the new one, and the old one you never answered.

Related Zap: 1. e4 e5 2. d4 exd4 3. Qxd4 d6 4. Nc3 Be6 5. Bb5 + Nd7 6. e5 dxe5 7. Qxe5 (Center Game).

Mating Net

1. e4	e6
2. d3	d5
3. Nd2	Nf6
4. g3	dxe4
5. dxe4	Bc5
6. Bg2	Nc6
7. Ne2?	Bxf2 + !
8. Kxf2	Ng4 +
9. Kf3?	

BLACK TO MOVE

Solution: It's mate, cruel and final, after **9. ... Nce5 +
10. Kf4 Qf6 + +**.

Comment: White's poorly placed knights on d2 and e2 are contributing factors in the loss. They obstruct freedom of movement, preventing White from defending properly. Place them on the third rank, where they are less obstructive and more powerful.

Related Zap: 1. d4 Nf6 2. c4 g6 3. Nc3 d5 4. cxd5 Nxd5 5. e3 Bg7 6. Bc4 Nb6 7. Bb3 c6 8. Nf3 N8d7 9. Bxf7 + Kxf7 10. Ng5 + Kf6 11. Nce4 + Kf5 12. g4 + + (Gruenfeld Defense).

FRENCH DEFENSE 142

Pin

1. e4	e6
2. f4	d5
3. e5	Be7
4. Qg4	g6
5. d4	Nh6
6. Qf3	Nf5
7. Qf2	b6
8. g4?	

BLACK TO MOVE

Solution: Black pins the queen with **8. . . . Bh4.**

Comment: Even in closed positions, when development is more deliberate, you still want to deploy your forces productively. Making five pawn moves and three queen moves is a sorry way to use the game's first eight moves. Throw in a blunder and it's over before it starts.

Related Zap: 1. e4 e5 2. Nf3 f5 3. Nxe5 Qf6 4. d4 d6 5. Nc4 fxe4 6. Be2 Be7 7. Nc3 Qg6 8. Bh5 (Latvian Gambit).

Related Zap: 1. e4 e5 2. Nf3 f6 3. Nxe5 Qe7 4. Nf3 Qxe4+ 5. Be2 Nc6 6. Nc3 Qg6 7. 0-0 Ne5 8. Nxe5 fxe5 9. Bh5 (Damiano Defense).

FRENCH DEFENSE 143

Fork

1.	e4	e6
2.	Nf3	d5
3.	e5	c5
4.	b4	cxb4
5.	d4	Nc6
6.	a3	Qa5
7.	Bd3	Nge7
8.	Nbd2?	b3
9.	cxb3?	

BLACK TO MOVE

Solution: The invasion **9. . . . Qc3!** forks rook and bishop.

Comment: White's play is superficial. The king should be taken off the a5-e1 diagonal before shifting the queen knight to d2. Then it wouldn't be pinned when Black pushes the b-pawn. Even as late as move nine, White could hold the fort by castling.

Related Zap: 1. d4 Nf6 2. Nf3 g6 3. b3 c5 4. Bb2 cxd4 5. Bxd4 Qa5+ 6. Bc3 Qh5 7. Nd2 Ne4 8. Qd3 Nxc3 9. Qxc3 (Queen Pawn Game).

FRENCH DEFENSE **144**

Fork

1. e4   e6
2. d4   b6
3. Qf3?   Nc6
4. d5   Nd4
5. Qc3?

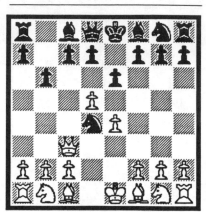

BLACK TO MOVE

Solution: The queen steps on a bad square: **5. . . . Bb4!
6. Qxb4,** and the knight forks king and queen, **6. . . . Nxc2 + .**

Comment: White's queen makes terrible use of two ideal squares—for knights. It goes to f3, thinly threatening a discovery to the queen rook. It shifts to c3 to defend c2. It gets pinned. It gets captured. It gets to start the next game back at d1.

Related Zap: 1. d4 c5 2. dxc5 Qa5+ 3. Nc3 Qxc5 4. e4 e5 5. Nf3 d6 6. Nd5 Nf6 7. b4 Qc6 8. Bb5 Qxb5 9. Nc7 + (Benoni Defense).

Double Threat

1. e4	e6
2. d4	Nf6
3. Bg5	Be7
4. Bd3	0-0
5. Nc3	Nxe4?
6. Bxe7	Nxc3

WHITE TO MOVE

Solution: The winning line is **7. Bxh7+! Kxh7 8. Qh5+ Kg8 9. Bxd8.** White also wins after **7. . . . Kh8 8. Qh5,** still threatening the queen and mate.

Comment: When both queens are menaced, the player who goes first usually has the advantage. It may be possible to save the queen with a gain of time (by giving check), while the opponent's queen remains under attack.

Related Zap: 1. e4 e6 2. d4 d5 3. Nc3 Nf6 4. e5 Nfd7 5. Bd3 Nb6 6. Qg4 N8d7 7. Bg5 Be7 8. Nf3 0-0 9. Qh4 (French Defense).

FRENCH DEFENSE **146**

Fork

1. e4   e6
2. d4   d5
3. f3   dxe4
4. fxe4?

BLACK TO MOVE

Solution: Black breezes ahead with **4. ... Qh4 +**.

Comment: It's a mistake for Black to check at h4 before exchanging on e4, for White can safely block on g3 without fear of losing the e-pawn. But after the exchange, e4 is no longer guarded and the queen can check and capture the pawn next move.

Related Zap: 1. e4 e5 2. f4 Bc5 3. fxe5 Qh4 + (King's Gambit Declined).

147

Trapping

1. e4   e6
2. d4   d5
3. exd5   exd5
4. Nf3   Bd6
5. c4   Ne7?

WHITE TO MOVE

Solution: The bishop is trapped by **6. c5.**

Comment: Black's fifth move puts the knight on an inferior square and leaves the bishop without a retreat. Exchanging pawns (5 . . . dxc4) solves the problem. If you want to be a survivor, be a responder. Answer enemy threats.

Related Zap: 1. d4 d5 2. e3 c5 3. Bd3 Nc6 4. Ne2 c4 (Colle Opening)

Related Zap: 1. d4 d5 2. f4 Be6 3. Qd3 Nd7 4. f5 (Stonewall Opening)

Related Zap: 1. d4 d5 2. c4 c6 3. Nf3 e6 4. Qc2 Bd6 5. Bg5 Ne7 6. g3 Qc7 7. c5 Qa5+ 8. Bd2 (Queen's Gambit Declined).

148

Trapping

1. e4	e6
2. d4	d5
3. exd5	exd5
4. Be3	Bd6
5. Qf3	c6
6. Nc3	Nf6
7. Bd3?	

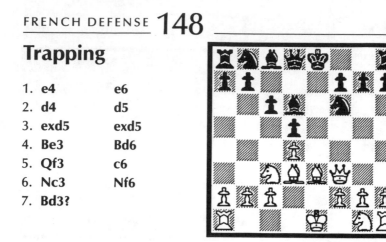

BLACK TO MOVE

Solution: The queen is gobbled up with **7. ... Bg4!**.

Comment: Moving the queen to f3 is generally a futile gesture. Sometimes this development is made for quick attack and to prepare queenside castling. But here it clashes with its own forces.

Related Zap: 1. d4 d5 2. Nf3 e6 3. Bf4 c6 4. e3 Nd7 5. Bd3 Qf6 6. Bg5 (Queen Pawn Game).

Mating Net

1.	e4	e6
2.	d4	d5
3.	Nd2	Nc6
4.	Ne2	e5
5.	exd5	Qxd5
6.	c4	Nb4
7.	cxd5?	

BLACK TO MOVE

Solution: A smothered end results from 7 . . . Nd3 + +.

Comment: Greed wins out. White takes the queen, paying no attention to Black's move (Nc6-b4), which threatens claustrophobic death. In general, don't position both your knights on the second rank.

Related Zap: 1. d4 d5 2. e3 Bf5 3. Nc3 Nc6 4. Bd2 Nf6 5. Ne2 Nb4 6. Rc1 Bxc2 7. Rxc2 Nd3 + + (Queen Pawn Game).

Related Zap: 1. e4 e5 2. Nf3 Nc6 3. Bb5 Nf6 4. d3 Ne7 5. Nxe5 c6 6. Nc4 cxb5 7. Nd6 + + (Ruy Lopez).

FRENCH DEFENSE 150

Jettison

1. **e4**	**e6**
2. **d4**	**d5**
3. **Nd2**	**c5**
4. **dxc5**	**Bxc5**
5. **exd5**	**exd5**
6. **Ne2?**	

BLACK TO MOVE

Solution: Black triumphs with **6. ... Qb6,** when White must jettison a knight to defend f2.

Comment: In the Tarrasch Variation of the French Defense, White develops a knight to d2, reserving the possibility of blocking a pinning attack along the a5-e1 diagonal by playing c2-c3. That explains the knight at d2. Nothing can justify placing the other knight at e2. It merely makes defense of f2 difficult.

Related Zap: 1. e4 e5 2. Nf3 d6 3. d4 Nbd7 4. c3 Ne7 5. dxe5 dxe5 6. Bc4 h6 7. Qb3 (Philidor Defense).

151

Fork

1. e4	e6
2. d4	d5
3. Nd2	c5
4. Ngf3	cxd4
5. Nxd4	Bc5
6. N2b3	dxe4?

WHITE TO MOVE

Solution: White gains a piece by **7. Bb5 + !,** when 7. . . . Bd7 fails to 8. Nxc5 Bxb5 9. Nxb7 Qb6 10. Nxb5. Black can't play 10. . . . Qxb5 because of 11. Nd6 + , forking king and queen.

Comment: Black lets the bishop hang (6. . . . dxe4?), hinging the defense on a forking queen check: 7. Nxc5 would be answered by 7. . . . Qa5 + and 8. . . . Qxc5. But White's surprise bishop check, 7. Bb5 + , closes the fifth rank and prevents defense. Look out for in-between moves, such as checks and captures. They can disrupt the course of events.

152

Trapping

1. **e4**	**e6**
2. **d4**	**d5**
3. **e5**	**f6**
4. **exf6**	**Qxf6**
5. **Nf3**	**b6**
6. **Bg5**	**Qg6**
7. **Bd3**	**Qf7?**

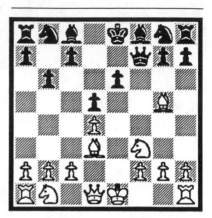

WHITE TO MOVE

Solution: Throw Black's queen in the trash after **8. Ne5!**.

Comment: Don't expect to accomplish much if you move only the queen and pawns. Make funeral arrangements when your opponent aims three minor pieces at your numerous weaknesses.

Related Zap: 1. d4 d5 2. c4 e6 3. Bf4 c6 4. e3 Be7 5. Bd3 Qd7 6. Nd2 Bd8 7. Nb3 Ne7 8. Nc5 (Queen Pawn Game).

153

Fork

1. e4   e6
2. d4   d5
3. e5   b6
4. c3   Ba6?

WHITE TO MOVE

Solution: The winning line is **5. Bxa6 Nxa6 6. Qa4+**.

Comment: Once White's c-pawn has moved, White has the possibility of a queen check at a4, with power sweeping along the a-file and the fourth rank. White wins a piece here by setting up the check with an exchange. (If 5. Qa4+?, then 5. . . . Qd7 saves the day.)

Related Zap: 1. d4 d5 2. c4 dxc4 3. e4 b5 4. a4 c6 5. axb5 cxb5 6. b3 Ba6 7. bxc4 bxc4 8. Rxa6 Nxa6 9. Qa4+ (Queen's Gambit Accepted).

Related Zap: 1. b3 e5 2. Ba3 Qh4 3. d3 Bxa3 4. Nxa3 Qb4+ (Nimzovich-Larsen Attack).

FRENCH DEFENSE **154**

Trapping

1.	e4	e6
2.	d4	d5
3.	e5	b6
4.	Bd3	c5
5.	Ne2?	

BLACK TO MOVE

Solution: White's bishop is lassoed by **5. . . . c4.**

Comment: The proper way for White to handle an attack on the base of his pawn chain (at d4) is to protect it with another pawn (5. c2-c3). Instead, White defends the d-pawn in a way that fails strategically as well as tactically. Pawns are the best protectors.

Related Zap: 1. e4 e5 2. f4 d6 3. Nc3 Be6 4. Nf3 Nd7 5. f5 (King's Gambit Declined).

Related Zap: 1. d3 d5 2. Bf4 e6 3. Nd2 Bd6 4. g3 e5 5. Be3 d4 (Mieses Opening).

Fork

1. e4	e6
2. d4	d5
3. e5	c5
4. c3	Nc6
5. Be3	Qb6
6. Qd2	Bd7
7. Nf3	Rc8
8. Bd3	cxd4
9. cxd4	Nb4
10. a3?	

BLACK TO MOVE

Solution: Black wins at least the exchange with **10. . . . Rc1 + !.** If the rook is taken, the knight takes the bishop, forking king and queen.

Comment: White's 10th move is an error. Castling instead is correct, losing the b-pawn after knight takes bishop. The b-pawn is vulnerable becuse of the premature development of the c1-bishop.

Related Zap: 1. d4 c5 2. d5 e5 3. Nc3 d6 4. g3 g6 5. Bh3 Bg7 6. Ne4 Nf6 7. Bxc8 (Benoni Defense).

156

Discovery

1. e4	e6
2. d4	d5
3. e5	c5
4. c3	Nc6
5. Nf3	Bd7
6. Bb5?	

BLACK TO MOVE

Solution: Black wins a pawn by the discovery **6. . . . Nxe5!**. If 7. Nxe5, then 7. . . . Bxb5. If 7. Bxd7 +, then 7. . . . Nxd7.

Comment: This is a typical tactic. Black can give up his knight because of the discovered attack on White's b5-bishop. Saving the bishop by taking on d7 allows the threatened knight to retreat to safety. So Black captures on e5 for free.

Related Zap: 1. e4 e5 2. Nc3 Nf6 3. Bc4 Nc6 4. d3 Nf6 5. Bg5 Be7 6. Nd5 Nxd5 (Vienna Game).

Discovery

1. **e4**	**e6**
2. **d4**	**d5**
3. **e5**	**c5**
4. **c3**	**Nc6**
5. **Nf3**	**Qb6**
6. **Bd3**	**cxd4**
7. **cxd4**	**Nxd4?**
8. **Nxd4**	**Qxd4?**

WHITE TO MOVE

Solution: White wins the queen by a discovery, **9. Bb5 +.** However Black gets out of check, White can take the queen.

Comment: Before taking the d-pawn (7. . . . Nxd4?), Black should prevent the possibility of a check along the a4-e8 diagonal by developing the bishop to d7. If White continues to offer the d-pawn, Black can then take it. Black would lose time, but not the queen.

Related Zap: 1. e4 e6 2. d4 d5 3. Bd3 dxe4 4. Bxe4 Nf6 5. Bd3 Qxd4 6. Bb5 + (French Defense).

Related Zap: 1. e4 e5 2. Nf3 Nc6 3. d4 exd4 4. Nxd4 Nxd4 5. Qxd4 c5 6. Qd2 d6 7. Bd3 d5 8. exd5 Qxd5 9. Bb5 + (Scotch Game).

158

Unpin

1. e4	e6
2. d4	d5
3. Nc3	c5
4. exd5	cxd4
5. Qxd4	Nf6
6. Bb5 +	Nc6?

WHITE TO MOVE

Solution: White wins by taking the knight, **7. dxc6!,** allowing the queen to be captured, **7. . . . Qxd4.** White gets the queen back after the discovered check, **8. cxb7 +,** gaining a rook in the bargain.

Comment: Black gets a little bit too cute. The d5-pawn is pinned and Black figures it can't move. But it can, and Black pays for this wrong assumption.

159

Trapping

1. e4	e6
2. d4	d5
3. Nc3	c5
4. Nf3	Nf6
5. e5	Nfd7
6. Bg5	Qb6
7. a3	Qxb2?

WHITE TO MOVE

Solution: White traps the queen with **8. Na4.**

Comment: When your opponent appears to ignore your threat, maybe a trap is being set. Here, White sets a trap with 7. a3, taking away the queen's potential escape squares.

Related Zap: 1. e4 c5 2. Nf3 d6 3. d4 cxd4 4. Nxd4 Nf6 5. Nc3 a6 6. Bg5 e6 7. f4 Qb6 8. a3 Qxb2 9. Na4 (Sicilian Defense).

Related Zap: 1. d4 d5 2. Bf4 c6 3. e3 Nf6 4. Nc3 Qb6 5. a3 Qxb2 6. Na4 (Queen Pawn Game).

Fork

1. e4	e6
2. d4	d5
3. Nc3	Nf6
4. Bg5	Bb4
5. e5	Bxc3 +
6. bxc3	h6
7. exf6	hxg5
8. fxg7	Rg8
9. Qh5	Rxg7?

WHITE TO MOVE

Solution: White vaporizes a rook with a forking queen check, **10. Qh8 +**.

Comment: Black blunders. Instead of taking the pawn on g7 with the rook, Black should attack the pawn again, playing the queen to f6. Then, on the next move, the pawn may be palatably eaten.

Related Zap: 1. e4 e5 2. Nf3 Nc6 3. d4 exd4 4. c3 d6 5. Bg5 Be7 6. h4 Bxg5 7. hxg5 f6 8. Qb3 fxg5 9. Rxh7 + Rxh7 10. Qxg8 + (Scotch Gambit).

Trapping

1. e4	e6
2. d4	d5
3. Nc3	Bb4
4. Bd3	c5
5. exd5	Qxd5
6. Nf3	cxd4
7. a3	Qa5?

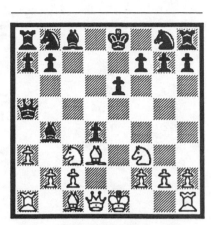

WHITE TO MOVE

Solution: White wins with **8. axb4! Qxa1 9. Nxd4,** and Black has no answer to the threat, 10. Nb3, trapping the meandering queen.

Comment: Better than the inadequate pin 7. . . . Qa5? is a direct exchange of bishop for knight (7. . . . Bxc3+). Instead, Black relies on the queen a little too much, and it walks into a blind alley.

Related Zap: 1. d4 d5 2. Nc3 e6 3. e3 Bb4 4. Nf3 c5 5. a3 cxd4 6. Nxd4 Qa5 7. axb4 Qxa1 8. Nb3 (Queen Pawn Game).

FRENCH DEFENSE **162**

Discovery

1.	e4	e6
2.	d4	d5
3.	Nc3	Bb4
4.	Bd2	dxe4
5.	Nxe4	Qxd4
6.	Bd3	Bxd2 +
7.	Qxd2	Qxb2
8.	Rd1	a6?

WHITE TO MOVE

Solution: White gets even with **9. Bb5 + !,** when blocking on c6 allows 10. Qd8 mate, and blocking on d7 lets White win a piece. If 9. . . . Ke7, then 10. Qd8 is mate.

Comment: Even with those pawn-grabbing exploits (5. . . . Qxd4 and 7. . . . Qxb2), Black would stay alive by avoiding the blunder 8. . . . a6, a move played to stop what it doesn't stop—a bishop check at b5.

Related Zap: 1. e4 e5 2. Nf3 h6 3. Nxe5 Qe7 4. d4 d6 5. Nf3 Qxe4 + 6. Be2 Bg4 7. 0-0 Kd8 8. Re1 a6 9. Bb5 (King Pawn Game).

163

Mating Net

1. **e4**	**e6**
2. **d4**	**d5**
3. **Nc3**	**Bb4**
4. **Bd2**	**dxe4**
5. **Qg4**	**Nf6**
6. **Qxg7**	**Rg8**
7. **Qh6**	**Qxd4**
8. **0-0-0**	**Ng4**
9. **Qh4**	**Nxf2**
10. **Nge2**	**Qb6**

WHITE TO MOVE

Solution: The beautiful sacrifice, **11. Qd8+!!**, forces mate: **11. . . . Kxd8 12. Bg5+ Ke8 13. Rd8++**.

Comment: Black's materialism, reliance on the queen, and precarious king position create problems. Instead of taking on f2, Black can hold the fort by retreating the bishop to e7, driving away the queen, or developing a minor piece to d7, closing the d-file.

Related Zap: 1. d4 d5 2. c4 c6 3. Nc3 e6 4. e4 dxe4 5. Nxe4 Bb4+ 6. Bd2 Qxd4 7. Nc3 a5 8. Qh5 Ra6 9. 0-0-0 Qxf2 10. Qg5 g6 11. Qd8+ Kxd8 12. Bg5+ Kc7 13. Bd8++ (Queen's Gambit Declined).

FRENCH DEFENSE 164

Mating Net

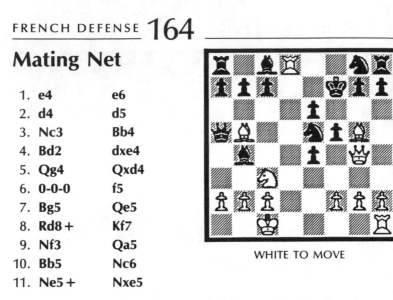

WHITE TO MOVE

1.	e4	e6
2.	d4	d5
3.	Nc3	Bb4
4.	Bd2	dxe4
5.	Qg4	Qxd4
6.	0-0-0	f5
7.	Bg5	Qe5
8.	Rd8+	Kf7
9.	Nf3	Qa5
10.	Bb5	Nc6
11.	Ne5+	Nxe5

Solution: It ends in mate via **12. Be8+ Kf8 13. Bg6++**.

Comment: A complicated vignette, with many interesting sidelines. The difference is that White is better developed, with forces poised for attack. Having four undeveloped pieces and an exposed king, Black offers poor resistance.

FRENCH DEFENSE 165

Pin

1. e4	e6
2. d4	d5
3. Nc3	Bb4
4. e5	b6
5. Qg4	Bf8
6. Bg5	Ne7
7. Bxe7!	Qxe7

WHITE TO MOVE

Solution: White confiscates a pawn, **8. Nxd5.** If 8. . . . exd5, then 9. Qxc8 + .

Comment: Black can keep the pawn with 6. . . . Qd7. The blocked center is the reason. You can get away with wasting time more often when the center is obstructed.

Related Zap: 1. e4 e6 2. d4 d5 3. Nc3 Nf6 4. Bg5 Be7 5. e5 Nfd7 6. h4 Bxg5 7. hxg5 Qxg5 8. Nh3 Qe7 9. Nf4 Nf8 10. Qg4 g6 11. Nfxd5 (French Defense).

Related Zap: 1. d4 d5 2. Qd3 e6 3. Qc3 c6 4. b3 Nd7 5. Ba3 Qg5 6. Bxf8 Qc1 + + (Queen Pawn Game).

Trapping

1. **e4**	**e6**
2. **d4**	**d5**
3. **Nc3**	**Bb4**
4. **e5**	**b6**
5. **Qg4**	**Bf8**
6. **Bg5**	**Qd7**
7. **0-0-0**	**h6**
8. **Bh4**	**g5**
9. **Bg3**	**h5**
10. **Qh3?**	

BLACK TO MOVE

Solution: No more queen after **10. . . . g4 11. Qh4 Be7.**

Comment: Usually it's good to lure enemy pawns forward so they become weak and hard to support. But make sure your own pieces don't become tangled in the advancing mass. Vulnerable pawns can still outnumber a queen.

Related Zap: 1. e4 e5 2. Bc4 Qh4 3. Nc3 Be7 4. d3 h6 5. Nd5 Bd8 6. g3 (Bishop's Opening).

Removing the Guard

1. e4	e6
2. d4	d5
3. Nc3	Bb4
4. e5	c5
5. a3	Ba5
6. b4	cxb4
7. Nb5	bxa3+
8. c3	Bc7
9. Bxa3	Ne7
10. Bd6	Na6

WHITE TO MOVE

Solution: Material is won: **11. Rxa6! bxa6 12. Nxc7+.**

Comment: White makes good use of the open lines, especially the a-file and the a3-f8 diagonal. White's grip on the dark squares, particularly d6, sets up the winning sacrifice. Usher's house, c7, falls.

Related Zap: 1. e4 b6 2. Nc3 Ba6 3. Bxa6 Nxa6 4. Qe2 Qc8 5. Nd5 Nf6 6. Qxa6 Qxa6 7. Nxc7+ (Owen Defense).

Double Threat

1. e4	e6
2. d4	d5
3. Nc3	Bb4
4. e5	c5
5. a3	Bxc3 +
6. bxc3	Ne7
7. Qg4	0-0
8. Bg5	Qc7
9. Bd3	c4?

WHITE TO MOVE

Solution: White wins a pawn with **10. Bxh7 + Kxh7 11. Qh4 + Kg8 12. Bxe7.**

Comment: When the center is closed and Black castles kingside, White often has shots against h7. Such sacrifices are more likely when the central barrier denies defensive access between the wings.

FRENCH DEFENSE 169

Trapping

1.	e4	e6
2.	d4	d5
3.	Nc3	Bb4
4.	e5	c5
5.	a3	Bxc3 +
6.	bxc3	Ne7
7.	a4	Qa5
8.	Qd2	Nc6
9.	Nf3	a6
10.	Ba3	Qxa4?

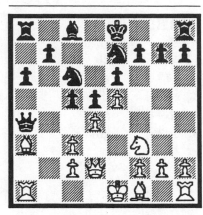

WHITE TO MOVE

Solution: The queen is won by **11. Bb2!**.

Comment: When the center is blocked by pawns, play tends to take place on the wings. In such cases, it's not uncommon to move the queen for a specific purpose, including pawn stealing. But don't go in when there's no way out.

Related Zap: 1. e4 e6 2. d4 d5 3. Nc3 Nf6 4. Bg5 Be7 5. e5 Nfd7 6. h4 Bxg5 7. hxg5 Qxg5 8. Nh3 Qh6 9. g3 a6 10. Bg2 f6 11. Nf4 Qg5 12. Rh5 (French Defense).

FRENCH DEFENSE **170**

Mating Net

1. **e4**	**e6**
2. **d4**	**d5**
3. **Nc3**	**dxe4**
4. **Nxe4**	**Ne7**
5. **Bd3**	**g6?**

WHITE TO MOVE

Solution: Black falls asleep. White stays awake, **6. Nf6 + +.**

Comment: It's necessary to move the e-pawn or the g-pawn to develop the f8-bishop. Moving both wastes a move and undefends f6, which is also weakened by placing the knight on e7. If you're going to flank your bishop, understand the ramifications of that setup before doing it.

Related Zap: 1. c4 Nc6 2. e3 d6 3. Ne2 Ne5 4. f4? Nd3 + + (English Opening).

Related Zap: 1. e4 d6 2. d4 Nf6 3. Nc3 g6 4. Nd5 Nxe4 5. Qe2 Nf6 6. Nxf6 + + (Pirc Defense).

171

Double Threat

1.	e4	e6
2.	d4	d5
3.	Nc3	dxe4
4.	Nxe4	Qd5
5.	Nc3	Bb4
6.	Qg4	Ne7
7.	Qxg7	Qe4 + ?

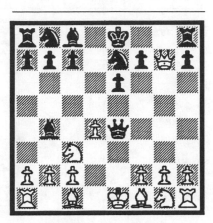

WHITE TO MOVE

Solution: White gives Black a headache with **8. Kd1!,** which leaves Black's queen and rook both hanging.

Comment: Black's best seventh move is 7. . . . Bxc3 +, followed by saving the h8-rook. Not all checks are good. Here, Black's queen check actually loses.

Skewer

1. **e4**	e6
2. **d4**	d5
3. **Nc3**	dxe4
4. **Nxe4**	c5
5. **c3**	f5
6. **Bg5**	Nf6
7. **Nxf6 +**	gxf6
8. **Qh5 +**	Ke7?

WHITE TO MOVE

Solution: White has a compound tactic winning the queen: **9. Bxf6 + ! Kxf6 10. Qh4 +**.

Comment: The f-pawn's rash strike on White's knight weakens the e8-h5 diagonal, and Black should block the attack on the queen with the bishop (6. . . . Be7). Even after these two slips, Black can still avoid the skewer with 8. . . . Kd7, if that's any consolation.

Related Zap: 1. e4 e5 2. f4 exf4 3. d3 Qh4 + 4. Ke2 d5 5. exd5 Bg4 + 6. Nf3 Bxf3 + 7. Kxf3 Qh5 + 8. g4 fxg3 + (King's Gambit Accepted).

173

Mating Net

1. e4	e6
2. d4	d5
3. Nc3	dxe4
4. Nxe4	Bd6
5. Bd3	Ne7
6. Bg5	0-0
7. Nf6+	gxf6
8. Bxf6	Qd7

WHITE TO MOVE

Solution: White has a forced mate in three moves: **9. Bxh7+!
Kxh7 10. Qh5+ Kg8 11. Qh8++.**

Comment: Black plays a number of second-rate moves, developing the dark-square bishop to d6, where it can be captured, putting the knight on e7, a square with little scope, and castling into White's attack, encouraging a bust-up sacrifice. Finally, Black misses the threat and allows mate. That's enough transgressions for any game.

Related Zap: 1. d4 d5 2. Nf3 Nf6 3. Bg5 e6 4. e3 Bb4+ 5. c3 Ba5 6. Ne5 Bb6 7. Bd3 0-0 8. Qf3 Nc6 9. Ng4 Ne7 10. Nxf6+ gxf6 11. Bxh7+ Kxh7 12. Qh5+ Kg7 13. Qh6+ Kg8 14. Bxf6 Nf5 15. Qh8++ (Queen Pawn Game).

FRENCH DEFENSE 174

Trapping

1. **e4**	**e6**
2. **d4**	**d5**
3. **Nc3**	**dxe4**
4. **Nxe4**	**Bd7**
5. **Nf3**	**Bc6**
6. **Bd3**	**Nf6**
7. **Nxf6 +**	**Qxf6?**
8. **Bg5**	**Bxf3**

WHITE TO MOVE

Solution: The winning move is **9. Qd2!,** protecting the bishop at g5 and roping Black's queen. If 9. . . . Qxd4, there follows 10. Bb5+ and 11. Qxd4.

Comment: Black could avoid queen loss by taking back on f6 with the g-pawn (7. . . . gxf6). Perhaps counting on removing the f3-knight (8. . . . Bxf3), counterattacking White's queen and thereby gaining the g5-bishop, Black misses 9. Qd2!.

Removing the Guard

1. e4	e6
2. d4	d5
3. Nc3	dxe4
4. Nxe4	Nd7
5. Nf3	Ngf6
6. Nxf6 +	Nxf6
7. Bd3	Be7
8. Qe2	0-0
9. Bg5	b6?

WHITE TO MOVE

Solution: White wins a piece with **10. Bxf6!.** If the bishop is taken back, White wins with 11. Qe4, threatening h7 and a8.

Comment: Black's queenside pawn move (9. . . . b6) is inopportune. Sometimes a downfall on the right side of the board stems from a weakness on the left. Try to induce weak points on both sides of the board and attack them simultaneously.

Related Zap: 1. d4 d5 2. c4 e6 3. Nf3 Nf6 4. Bg5 Be7 5. e3 0-0 6. Nbd2 b6 7. Bd3 Nc6 8. cxd5 Nb4 9. Bb1 exd5 10. a3 Nc6 11. Bxf6 Bxf6 12. Qc2 (Queen's Gambit Declined).

FRENCH DEFENSE **176**

Double Threat

1. **e4**	**e6**
2. **d4**	**d5**
3. **Nc3**	**dxe4**
4. **Nxe4**	**b6**
5. **Qf3**	**c6**
6. **Bg5**	**Qxd4?**
7. **Rd1**	**Qb4 +**

WHITE TO MOVE

Solution: After **8. c3,** Black must give up the queen; otherwise, White mates at d8.

Comment: Black's pawn-grabbing backfires. In the final position, White has four developed pieces to Black's one—the queen. That's why Black loses it.

Related Zap: 1. e4 e5 2. Nf3 d6 3. d4 Qf6 4. Nc3 Be6 5. dxe5 dxe5 6. Bg5 (Philidor Defense).

Trapping

1.	e4	e6
2.	d4	d5
3.	Nc3	dxe4
4.	Nxe4	b6
5.	Nf3	Bb7
6.	Bb5	Nd7
7.	Ne5	Bc8?
8.	Bg5	f6

WHITE TO MOVE

Solution: White's pieces are forked, but Black's queen is trapped, **9. Nc6!.**

Comment: Flanking the queen bishop weakens c6. Retreating the bishop back to c8 abandons c6 to White's marauders. After White forces a closing of the queen's diagonal (8. Bg5 f6), the knight invades on c6 to do its dirty work.

Related Zap: 1. d4 d5 2. Nf3 b6 3. Ne5 Nd7 4. Nc6 (Queen Pawn Game)

Related Zap: 1. e4 e5 2. f4 d5 3. exd5 e4 4. Bc4 Nf6 5. Nc3 Bb4 6. Nge2 Ng4 7. Nxe4 Ne3 (Falkbeer Counter Gambit).

Skewer

1. e4	e6
2. d4	d5
3. Nc3	dxe4
4. Nxe4	Nf6
5. Nxf6+	Qxf6
6. Nf3	h6
7. g3	g6
8. Bf4	c6?

WHITE TO MOVE

Solution: Black's dark squares are skewered, **9. Be5.**

Comment: Black could avoid material loss on move eight by Qf6-d8 or Bf8-d6 but plays mechanically and misses White's deeper threat. A sign of impending doom is that after eight moves the queen is Black's only developed piece.

Related Zap: 1. e4 d5 2. exd5 Qxd5 3. d4 b6 4. Be2 Qxg2 5. Bf3 (Center Counter Defense).

Related Zap: 1. c4 c5 2. Nf3 Nf6 3. Nc3 g6 4. d3 b6 5. Bd2 e6 6. Ne4 Bb7 7. Nxf6+ Qxf6 8. Bc3 (English Opening).

Discovery

1.	e4	e6
2.	d4	d5
3.	Nc3	dxe4
4.	Nxe4	Nf6
5.	Bd3	Qxd4?

WHITE TO MOVE

Solution: Another pawn, another gain of the queen by discovery: **6. Bb5 +.** if 6. . . . Nc6, then 7. Qxd4.

Comment: If your opponent lets you take a free pawn with your queen—correction, purposely refrains from defending it—don't take it before you've made sure there isn't a trick. Otherwise, like magic, your queen disappears.

Related Zap: 1. e4 e5 2. Nf3 Nf6 3. Nxe5 Qe7 4. Nf3 Qxe4 + 5. Be2 d6 6. 0-0 Nc6 7. Re1 Ne5 8. Bb5 + (Petrov Defense).

Fork

1. e4	e6
2. d4	d5
3. Nc3	dxe4
4. Nxe4	Nf6
5. Bd3	Nxe4
6. Bxe4	c5
7. c3	cxd4
8. cxd4	Bb4+
9. Bd2	Qxd4?

WHITE TO MOVE

Solution: Win a piece with **10. Qa4+ Nc6 11. Bxc6+ bxc6 12. Qxb4.**

Comment: White's d-pawn can't be taken because it has an indirect defense—the queen check at a4. Very often Black can answer this shot by developing the knight to c6, blocking the check and defending the bishop. But here the knight is captured with check, removing the bishop's protection.

Related Zap: 1. c4 e5 2. g3 Bb4 3. Bg2 d6 4. Qa4+ Nc6 5. Bxc6+ bxc6 6. Qxb4 (English Opening).

FRENCH DEFENSE **181**

Trapping

1. **e4**	**e6**
2. **d4**	**d5**
3. **Nc3**	**dxe4**
4. **Nxe4**	**Nf6**
5. **Bd3**	**Nc6**
6. **Nf3**	**a6?**
7. **Nxf6 +**	**Qxf6?**

WHITE TO MOVE

Solution: Black's queen is caught by **8. Bg5.**

Comment: Black's sixth move is pointless and the seventh move blunderous. But play 7. . . . gxf6, and Black's still in the game. With 7. . . . Qxf6?, Black avoids doubled pawns for the price of a queen.

Related Zap: 1. d4 d5 2. Nf3 e6 3. Bf4 Qf6 4. e3 c5 5. Bd3 c4 6. Bg5 (Queen Pawn Game).

Related Zap: 1. d4 Nf6 2. c4 e6 3. Nc3 Bb4 4. Nf3 0-0 5. Bf4 Ne4 6. Rc1 c5 7. e3 Qf6 8. Bd3 Nxc3 9. bxc3 Ba3 10. Bg5 (Nimzo-Indian Defense).

Discovery

1. **e4**	**e6**
2. **d4**	**d5**
3. **Nc3**	**dxe4**
4. **Nxe4**	**Nf6**
5. **Bd3**	**Nc6**
6. **Nf3**	**Nxd4**
7. **Nxd4**	**Qxd4?**

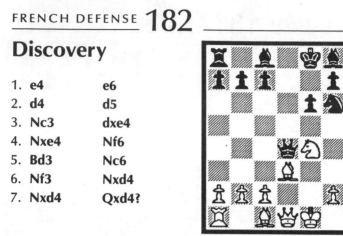

WHITE TO MOVE

Solution: White wins the queen with **8. Bb5 +**.

Comment: It's unlikely that your opponent will let the d-pawn hang without a reason. The reason turns out to be a stinger that gains the queen. Black should simply develop the king bishop to e7 and prepare castling. As the sages say: development is better than riches.

Related Zap: 1. e4 e6 2. d4 d5 3. Nd2 c5 4. exd5 exd5 5. dxc5 Bxc5 6. Nb3 Bd6 7. Qxd5 Bb4 + (French Defense).

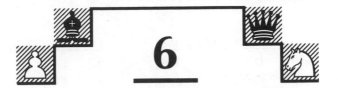

6

CENTER COUNTER DEFENSE

(TRAPS 183-217)

1. e4 d5

TRAPS	WHITE'S 2ND MOVE	BLACK'S 2ND MOVE
183	2. Nc3	2. . . . dxe4
184	2. Nc3	2. . . . d4
185-189	2. exd5	2. . . . Nf6
190-217	2. exd5	2. . . . Qxd5

continued

TRAPS	WHITE'S 3RD MOVE	BLACK'S 3RD MOVE
190	3. Ke2	3. . . . Qe4+ +
191	3. Ne2	3. . . . Bg4
192	3. d4	3. . . . Nc6
193	3. d4	3. . . . Nd7
194-195	3. d4	3. . . . Nf6
196	3. Nc3	3. . . . Qc6
197	3. Nc3	3. . . . Qe5+
198	3. Nc3	3. . . . Qc5
199	3. Nc3	3. . . . Qd7
200	3. Nc3	3. . . . Qd6
201-202	3. Nc3	3. . . . Qg5
203-205	3. Nc3	3. . . . Qd8
206-217	3. Nc3	3. . . . Qa5

183

Mating Net

1. **e4**	d5
2. **Nc3**	dxe4
3. **Nxe4**	Nd7
4. **Nf3**	c5
5. **Bb5**	a6
6. **Qe2**	axb5?

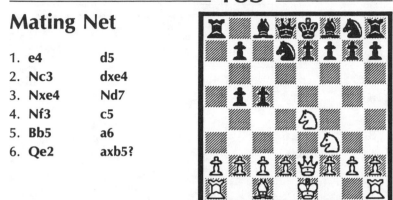

WHITE TO MOVE

Solution: Black is undeniably mated by **7. Nd6+ +.**

Comment: Playing the knight to d7 blocks the Black queen's defense of d6, and advancing the c-pawn relinquishes control of d6. White puts the queen on e2 so the e-pawn will be pinned and unable to guard d6. Finally, White's knight mates on d6.

Related Zap: 1. c4 e5 2. Nf3 Nc6 3. g3 Nd4 4. Nxe5 Qe7 5. Nd3 Nf3+ + (English Opening).

CENTER COUNTER DEFENSE **184**

Direct Attack

1. e4	d5
2. Nc3	d4
3. Nce2	e5
4. Ng3	c5
5. Bc4	Nc6
6. Nf3	Nf6?

WHITE TO MOVE

Solution: The f-pawn is history after **7. Ng5!**.

Comment: Black should delay the development of the king knight in favor of moving the king bishop. With 6. . . . Be7, Black stops Nf3-g5, then on move seven can develop the king knight and follow up by castling on move eight, position intact.

Related Zap: 1. e4 e5 2. Nf3 Nc6 3. Bb5 a6 4. Ba4 Nge7 5. d3 b5 6. Bb3 Ng6 7. Ng5 (Ruy Lopez).

Unpin

1. e4	d5
2. exd5	Nf6
3. c4	c6
4. dxc6	Nxc6
5. d3	e5
6. Nc3	Bc5
7. Bg5	0-0
8. Ne4?	

BLACK TO MOVE

Solution: Black wins a piece with **8. . . . Nxe4!**. If 9. Bxd8, then 8. . . . Bxf2+ 9. Ke2 Nd4++.

Comment: White pushes the attack even though Black is better developed and more prepared. If you try to overtake a fortified position it will get you. White's king is no match for Black's three minor pieces.

Related Zap: 1. e4 e5 2. Bc4 Nf6 3. Nf3 Nxe4 4. Nc3 Nxc3 5. dxc3 d6 6. 0-0 Bg4 7. Nxe5 Bxd1 8. Bxf7+ Ke7 9. Bg5++ (Bishop's Opening).

CENTER COUNTER DEFENSE 186

Saving

1.	e4	d5
2.	exd5	Nf6
3.	Bb5 +	Bd7
4.	Bc4	Bg4
5.	Nf3	Nxd5
6.	Nc3	Nxc3
7.	Bxf7 + ?	Kxf7
8.	Ne5 +	Kg8
9.	Qxg4	

BLACK TO MOVE

Solution: With **9. . . . Qd5!**, Black keeps the extra piece.

Comment: Good defensive moves can be hard to find. Black's terrific queen move, 9. . . . Qd5!, stops mate at e6 while gaining time. If White takes Black's knight at c3, Black takes White's knight, at e5.

Related Zap: 1. d4 d5 2. c4 e6 3. Nc3 c5 4. Nf3 cxd4 5. Nxd4 e5 6. Nf3 d4 7. Nxe5 Qd6 (Queen's Gambit Declined).

187

Overload

1. e4	d5
2. exd5	Nf6
3. d4	Nxd5
4. c4	Nb6
5. Nf3	Bg4
6. c5	Nd5
7. Qb3	b6
8. Ne5!	Be6

WHITE TO MOVE

Solution: The deadly **9. Bb5 +** puts Black in a quandary. Blocking with the c-pawn loses to 10. Nxc6, while 9. . . . Nd7 10. Bxd7 + wins the knight at d5.

Comment: Black is ruined by glaring weaknesses on the light squares and obstructing pieces that stumble into each other. White's knight on e5 watches imperiously over the debacle.

188

Mating Net

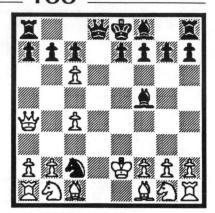

1. e4	d5
2. exd5	Nf6
3. d4	Nxd5
4. c4	Nb4
5. Qa4+	N8c6
6. d5	Bf5
7. dxc6?	Nc2+
8. Ke2?	

BLACK TO MOVE

Solution: The only mate is **8. . . . Qd3+ +.**

Comment: Taking the knight on c6 is suicide. Having taken it, White should sacrifice the queen (8. Qxc2) to stop the mate. In the end, White moves only two pieces: the king and queen. This is a good formula for losing chess games.

Related Zap: 1. d4 Nf6 2. c4 g6 3. g3 Bg7 4. Bg2 d5 5. cxd5 Nxd5 6. e4 Nb4 7. Qa4+ N8c6 8. d5 Nd3+ 9. Kf1 Nxc1 10. dxc6 b5 11. Qc2 Bxb2 (Gruenfeld Defense).

Trapping

1. e4	d5
2. exd5	Nf6
3. d4	Nxd5
4. c4	Nb4
5. Qa4 +	N8c6
6. a3	Na6
7. d5	Nc5
8. Qb5	b6
9. Qxc6 + ?	

BLACK TO MOVE

Solution: Black blocks the check, **9.... Bd7,** and wins the queen!

Comment: In the Center Counter Defense, it's usually Black who moves the queen too much. Here, it's White. In the final position, after nine moves, White has developed only one piece: the queen.

Related Zap: 1. e4 d5 2. exd5 Nf6 3. d4 Nxd5 4. c4 Nb4 5. Qa4 + N8c6 6. a3 Na6 7. d5 Nc5 8. Qb5 b6 9. dxc6 a5 10. b4 Ba6 (Center Counter Defense).

CENTER COUNTER DEFENSE **190**

Mating Net

1. e4   d5
2. exd5   Qxd5
3. Ke2?

BLACK TO MOVE

Solution: It's mate most cruel, **3. . . . Qe4 + +!**.

Comment: White didn't blunder but was called for "touch move" and had to play the touched king. Keep your hands off your pieces until you're sure of your move. One mistake can throw away a great game. Have a nice day.

Related Zap: 1. e4 e5 2. f4 exf4 3. Nf3 g5 4. Bc4 f6 5. Nxg5 fxg5 6. Qh5+ Ke7 7. Qf7+ Kd6 8. Qd5+ Ke7 9. Qe5+ + (King's Gambit Accepted).

Fork

1.	e4	d5
2.	exd5	Qxd5
3.	Ne2	Bg4
4.	Nbc3	Bxe2
5.	Bxe2	Qxg2?

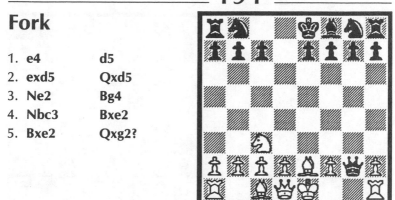

WHITE TO MOVE

Solution: White wins at least a rook with **6. Bf3.**

Comment: White's winning move, 6. Bf3, combines attack and defense. It deals with Black's threat and gains time. It also introduces a threat of White's: to take on b7. Black has no answer to White's two-front assault.

Related Zap: 1. e4 e5 2. Nf3 Nc6 3. d4 exd4 4. Nxd4 Qh4 5. Nb5 Qxe4+ 6. Be2 Qxg2 7. Bf3 (Scotch Game).

CENTER COUNTER DEFENSE **192**

Removing the Guard

1. e4	d5
2. exd5	Qxd5
3. d4	Nc6
4. Nf3	Bg4
5. Be2	Bxf3
6. Bxf3	Qxd4?

WHITE TO MOVE

Solution: Oops! Goodbye queen: **7. Bxc6+ bxc6 8. Qxd4.**

Comment: Black wouldn't be so badly off were it not for the loss of the queen. Black has adequate development and is ready to castle queenside. But White has the move, and that's the difference.

Related Zap: 1. c4 e5 2. Nc3 c6 3. g3 d5 4. cxd5 cxd5 5. d4 exd4 6. Qxd4 Nf6 7. Bg5 Be7 8. Bxf6 Bxf6 9. Qxd5 Bxc3+ 10. bxc3 Qxd5 (English Opening).

Double Threat

1.	e4	d5
2.	exd5	Qxd5
3.	d4	Nd7
4.	c4	Qd6
5.	Nf3	c5
6.	Be2	Nb6?
7.	b4	cxd4
8.	c5	Qf6

WHITE TO MOVE

Solution: After **9. Bg5!,** White can take the b6-knight without risk.

Comment: Black's defense is based on a trick. If White immediately takes the knight, 9. cxb6, Black plays 9. . . . d3, hitting e2 and a1. But 9. Bg5 drives away the queen, preventing the discovery. The knight Is then taken for free.

Related Zap: 1. d4 d5 2. c4 Nc6 3. Nc3 Be6 4. e4 dxe4 5. d5 (Queen's Gambit Declined).

CENTER COUNTER DEFENSE 194

Saving

1.	e4	d5
2.	exd5	Qxd5
3.	d4	Nf6
4.	Nc3	Bg4?

WHITE TO MOVE

Solution: White wins at least a piece with **5. Nxd5 Bxd1 6. Nxf6 +**. White also wins a piece with 5. Qxg4 Nxg4 6. Nxd5.

Comment: In queen-for-queen situations, the player who goes first usually has an enormous advantage. That player may be able to save the queen with a check and then take the opponent's for free. Or, by virtue of going first, the first player may simply be able to capture more. That's what happens here.

Related Zap: 1. c4 e5 2. e3 d5 3. cxd5 Qxd5 4. Ne2 Bg4 5. Nec3 Bxd1 6. Nxd5 (English Opening).

Removing the Guard

1.	e4	d5
2.	exd5	Qxd5
3.	d4	Nf6
4.	c4	Qe4+
5.	Ne2	e5
6.	Nc3	Bb4
7.	Qa4+	Nc6
8.	d5	Nxd5!
9.	cxd5?	

BLACK TO MOVE

Solution: White's queen goes: **9. . . . Bxc3 +! 10. bxc3 Qxa4.**

Comment: White thinks that advancing the d-pawn wins a piece. It seems that Black is trying to limit the damage by capturing on d5, but the idea is to clear the line to set up a discovery, queen to queen. It works like a charm.

Related Zap: 1. d4 d5 2. c4 e6 3. Nc3 Nf6 4. Nf3 Bb4 5. Qa4+ Nc6 6. cxd5 Qxd5 7. g3 Qc4 8. e4 Bxc3+ (Queen's Gambit Declined).

CENTER COUNTER DEFENSE 196

Pin

1. e4   d5
2. exd5   Qxd5
3. Nc3   Qc6?

WHITE TO MOVE

Solution: The pin **4. Bb5** wins the queen.

Comment: This is a classic case of bringing out the queen early and running into trouble. Either retreating the queen to d8 or shifting it to a5 is better than the blunder 3. . . . Qc6?. Have it your way.

Related Zap: 1. e4 e5 2. Nf3 d6 3. d4 Bg4 4. dxe5 Bxf3 5. Qxf3 dxe5 6. Bc4 Nf6 7. Qb3 Qd7 8. Qxb7 Qc6 9. Bb5 (Philidor Defense).

Related Zap: 1. e4 e5 2. d4 exd4 3. Qxd4 Nc6 4. Qc3 Bb4 (Center Game).

Fork

1.	e4	d5
2.	exd5	Qxd5
3.	Nc3	Qe5+
4.	Ne2	Nc6
5.	d4	Qe6?

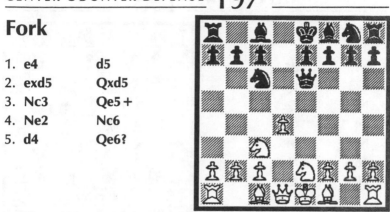

WHITE TO MOVE

Solution: Fork Black and win a knight: **6. d5!**.

Comment: Yuch! Three queen moves in the first five plays. The queen check at e5 is pointless, forcing White to develop a new piece. Putting the queen on e6, even if it didn't lose a piece, would be bad, for it blocks the e-pawn and the c8-bishop. In the opening, rely on center pawns and minor pieces, not the queen.

Related Zap: 1. e4 Nf6 2. e5 Nd5 3. d4 g6 4. c4 Nb6 5. Be2 d6 6. exd6 Qxd6 7. c5 (Alekhine Defense).

Discovery

1. **e4**	**d5**
2. **exd5**	**Qxd5**
3. **Nc3**	**Qc5**
4. **d4**	**Qa5**
5. **Nf3**	**Bf5**
6. **Ne5**	**Nc6**
7. **Nc4**	**Qa6**

WHITE TO MOVE

Solution: White unveils a winning discovery to Black's queen, **8. Nd6 + !**.

Comment: You can't expect much good to ensue from four early queen moves. White's S.W.A.T. force of minor pieces and central pawn bring down the misused, misplaced enemy queen.

Pin

1. **e4**	**d5**
2. **exd5**	**Qxd5**
3. **Nc3**	**Qd7?**
4. **Nf3**	**c5?**
5. **d4**	**Nc6?**
6. **d5**	**Nd4**
7. **Nxd4**	**cxd4**

WHITE TO MOVE

Solution: Let's pin Black's queen: **8. Bb5.**

Comment: Black plays three inferior moves in a row: retreating the queen to d7, advancing the c-pawn so that it can't block on c6, and developing the knight where it can be menaced by a pawn. It usually takes several bad moves to lose a game. Black qualifies.

CENTER COUNTER DEFENSE 200

Trapping

1. **e4**	**d5**
2. **exd5**	**Qxd5**
3. **Nc3**	**Qd6**
4. **d4**	**Nf6**
5. **Bg5**	**a6**
6. **Nf3**	**Nc6**
7. **d5**	**Nb4?**
8. **Bxf6**	**exf6**

WHITE TO MOVE

Solution: Black's knight is dead in the water after **9. a3.**

Comment: Black prevents the queen from being attacked by playing 5. . . . a6. But the pawn that occupies the square a6 prevents the knight on b4 from retreating there. So playing the knight to b4 is a blunder.

Related Zap: 1. e4 e5 2. Nf3 Nf6 3. d4 exd4 4. Bd3 h6 5. e5 Ng4 6. h3 (Petrov Defense).

Trapping

1. e4	d5
2. exd5	Qxd5
3. Nc3	Qg5
4. d4	Qg6
5. Bd3	Qxg2

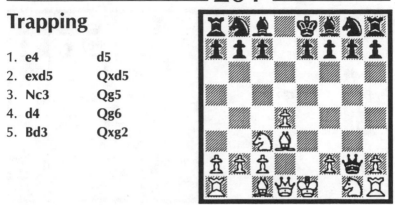

WHITE TO MOVE

Solution: White subdues with **6. Be4!**, trapping the queen.

Comment: Black can try 6. . . . Bg4, attacking White's queen. White then wins by moving the queen to d2 or d3, or by taking Black's queen, leading to the gain of Black's light-square bishop.

Related Zap: 1. e4 e6 2. d4 Qh4 3. Bd3 h5 4. Nf3 Qg4 5. h3 Qxg2 6. Rg1 Qxh3 7. Bf1 (French Defense).

CENTER COUNTER DEFENSE 202

Mating Net

1. **e4**	**d5**
2. **exd5**	**Qxd5**
3. **Nc3**	**Qg5**
4. **d4**	**Qg6**
5. **Bd3**	**Bf5**
6. **Qf3**	**Bxd3**
7. **Qxb7**	**Qc6?**

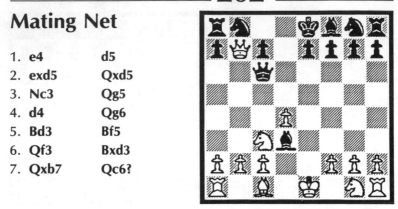

WHITE TO MOVE

Solution: If you're tired of this game, mate with **8. Qc8 + +.**

Comment: Black moves his queen too much (four of seven moves) and pays for it. In the final position, Black guards the vulnerable a8-h1 diagonal but not the undefended square c8. It's hard to survive if you don't move a thing kingside.

Related Zap: 1. e4 e6 2. d4 d5 3. e5 c5 4. Qg4 cxd4 5. Nf3 f5 6. Qg3 Nc6 7. Be2 Bd7 8. Nxd4 Nxd4 9. Bh5 + Ke7 10. Qa3 + + (French Defense).

Unpin

1. e4	d5
2. exd5	Qxd5
3. Nc3	Qd8
4. d4	Nc6
5. Nf3	Bg4
6. d5	Ne5
7. Nxe5!	Bxd1
8. Bb5+	c6
9. dxc6	a6

WHITE TO MOVE

Solution: White maintains the edge with **10. c7+! axb5 11. cxd8(Q)+ Rxd8 12. Nxd1.**

Comment: Keep a sharp lookout when piling up on pinned knights that can fend for themselves. When the pinning piece is the queen bishop, be especially alert to unpinning combinations.

CENTER COUNTER DEFENSE 204

Mating Net

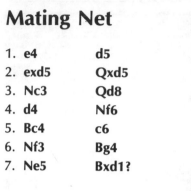

1.	**e4**	d5
2.	**exd5**	Qxd5
3.	**Nc3**	Qd8
4.	**d4**	Nf6
5.	**Bc4**	c6
6.	**Nf3**	Bg4
7.	**Ne5**	Bxd1?

WHITE TO MOVE

Solution: The end is **8. Bxf7 + +.**

Comment: Black doesn't have to lose anything. Instead of taking the queen, Black can withdraw the bishop to e6. True, White can exchange bishops, doubling Black's e-pawns and gaining a definite edge. But there's no mate, and that's what matters.

Related Zap: 1. e4 e6 2. d4 d5 3. Nc3 c5 4. exd5 exd5 5. Bb5 + Nc6 6. Nf3 Nf6 7. Ne5 Qc7 8. Bg5 Ne4 9. Nxd5 Qd6 10. Bh4 Qxd5 11. Bc4 Qxd4 12. Bxf7 + + (French Defense).

205

Unpin

1. e4	d5
2. exd5	Qxd5
3. Nc3	Qd8
4. d4	Nf6
5. Bc4	c6
6. Nf3	Bg4
7. Bxf7+	Kxf7

WHITE TO MOVE

Solution: White gets back the piece and winds up a pawn ahead, **8. Ne5+ Kg8 9. Nxg4.**

Comment: When unpinning the knight, the unpinner has a dilemma. Is it better to sacrifice on f7 first (1. Bc4xf7+) and then move the knight (2. Nf3-e5+), or to move the knight first (1. Ne5), threatening mate with the bishop (2. Bxf7++)? The decision must be based on concrete analysis.

CENTER COUNTER DEFENSE 206

Fork

1. **e4**	**d5**
2. **exd5**	**Qxd5**
3. **Nc3**	**Qa5**
4. **Bc4**	**g6**
5. **Qf3**	**Nf6**
6. **Nd5**	**Bg7**

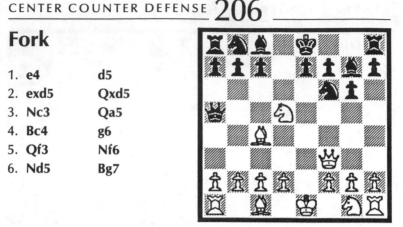

WHITE TO MOVE

Solution: White wins gobs of material with **7. b4! Qa4 8. Bb5 +! Qxb5 9. Nxc7 +.**

Comment: Black's flanking of the king bishop is a mistake. There's no time for that. Developing the king knight is more in tune with the proceedings. To get out the king bishop, Black should advance the e-pawn one square, which also blocks out White's king bishop.

Related Zap: 1. e4 e6 2. d4 d5 3. Nd2 c5 4. dxc5 Bxc5 5. Qg4 Nf6 6. Qxg7 Rg8 7. Qh6 Bxf2 + 8. Kxf2 Ng4 + (French Defense).

Double Threat

1. e4	d5
2. exd5	Qxd5
3. Nc3	Qa5
4. Bb5+	Nc6?
5. Bxc6+	bxc6
6. Nf3	c5?
7. Ne5	Ba6?

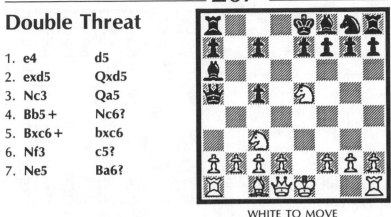

WHITE TO MOVE

Solution: White's **8. Qf3!** is a crusher. Black cannot defend a8, c6, and f7 all with one move.

Comment: Black forgets about the kingside, where nothing gets moved. First accepting horrible weaknesses, Black actually exposes them by advancing the doubled pawn, then displaces the queen so it can't lend a hand when needed. What a soap opera.

CENTER COUNTER DEFENSE 208

Mating Net

1. **e4**	**d5**
2. **exd5**	**Qxd5**
3. **Nc3**	**Qa5**
4. **Nf3**	**e5**
5. **d3**	**Bg4**
6. **Bd2**	**Nc6**
7. **Qe2**	**Nd4**
8. **Qxe5 + ?**	**Qxe5**
9. **Nxe5**	

BLACK TO MOVE

Solution: The check **9. . . . Nxc2 + +** is a mating one.

Comment: White goes pawn-grabbing with the queen and Black goes king-grabbing with the minor pieces. Don't play the opening to win pawns. That's playing for peanuts, and best left to other members of our glorious simian heritage.

Related Zap: 1. e4 c5 2. b4 cxb4 3. Bb2 Nc6 4. d4 d5 5. exd5 Qxd5 6. c4 bxc3 7. Nxc3 Qxd4 8. Nd5 Qxb2 9. Nc7 + + (Sicilian Defense).

CENTER COUNTER DEFENSE **209**

Trapping

1. e4	d5
2. exd5	Qxd5
3. Nc3	Qa5
4. d4	Qb6
5. a3	Nf6
6. Be3	Qxb2?

WHITE TO MOVE

Solution: The queen is trapped by **7. Na4.**

Comment: What should Black expect? If four of the first six moves are made with the queen, there are no resources to draw upon when needed. In the end, Black needs a miracle.

Related Zap: 1. d4 d5 2. Nf3 Bf5 3. e3 Nc6 4. c3 e6 5. Qb3 a6 6. Qxb7 Na5 (Queen Pawn Game).

CENTER COUNTER DEFENSE **210**

Fork

1. e4	d5
2. exd5	Qxd5
3. Nc3	Qa5
4. d4	e5
5. dxe5	Bb4
6. Bd2	Nc6
7. a3	Nd4
8. axb4?	

BLACK TO MOVE

Solution: Black wins the exchange with **8. . . . Qxa1!**. If **9. Qxa1**, then **9. . . . Nxc2+** regains the queen.

Comment: Black's tactic is based on luring White's queen a knight's jump away from c2. The queen sacrifice 8. . . . Qxa1 is only an investment, since Black gets the queen back plus some goodies in the bargain.

Related Zap: 1. d4 d5 2. c4 Nf6 3. cxd5 Nxd5 4. e4 Nb4 5. Nc3 Qxd4 6. Qxd4 Nc2+ (Queen's Gambit Declined).

Desperado

1. e4	d5
2. exd5	Qxd5
3. Nc3	Qa5
4. d4	e5
5. Nf3	Bg4
6. Be2	Nc6
7. Nxe5	Bxe2
8. Nxc6?	

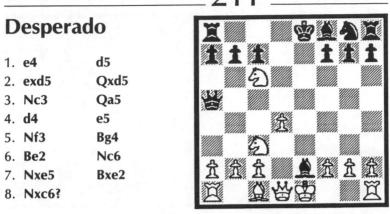

BLACK TO MOVE

Solution: Black wins a piece by **8. . . . Qxc3 + !! 9. bxc3 Bxd1.**

Comment: Black's queen sacrifice is called a desperado. Since both queens are threatened and Black has the move, Black gets something for the queen (the knight at c3), sweetening the deal. White doesn't get anything for his. This is basic chess capitalism.

Related Zap: 1. d4 d5 2. c4 c6 3. cxd5 cxd5 4. Nf3 Nf6 5. Nc3 Nc6 6. Qd3 g6 7. e4 dxe4 8. Nxe4 Nxe4 9. Qxe4 Qa5 + 10. Bd2 Bf5 11. Qxc6 + (Queen's Gambit Declined).

Related Zap: 1. d4 Nf6 2. c4 g6 3. g3 d5 4. e3 Nc6 5. cxd5 Qxd5 6. Qf3 Qa5 + 7. Bd2 Bg4 8. Qxc6 + (Gruenfeld Defense).

Fork

1. e4	d5
2. exd5	Qxd5
3. Nc3	Qa5
4. d4	Nf6
5. Bc4	Bf5
6. Bd2	e6?
7. Nd5!	Qa4

WHITE TO MOVE

Solution: The queen goes, **8. Bb5 + ! Qxb5 9. Nxc7 + .**

Comment: White's 6. Bd2 has two points: to break the pin and to free the knight to move. Black doesn't appreciate this second point, and the discovery 7. Nd5! seems to win a rook. But as Black soon learns, it actually wins the queen.

Related Zap: 1. e4 e5 2. d4 exd4 3. Qxd4 Nc6 4. Qa4 Bc5 5. Bc4 d6 6. Bd5 Bd7 7. Nf3 Nd4 8. Qc4 Bb5 9. Qc3 Bb4 10. Qxb4 Nxc2 + (Center Game).

Trapping

1.	e4	d5
2.	exd5	Qxd5
3.	Nc3	Qa5
4.	d4	Nf6
5.	Nf3	c6
6.	Ne5	Nbd7
7.	Nc4	Qb4?

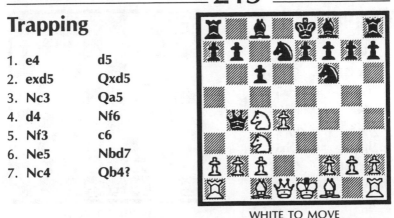

WHITE TO MOVE

Solution: The quiet advance **8. a3** snares the queen.

Comment: If you rely on one piece too much, you run the risk of losing that piece. Black's queen is like Custer at Little Big Horn: surrounded, outnumbered, and without a prayer.

Related Zap: 1. e4 e5 2. Nf3 Nc6 3. d4 exd4 4. Nxd4 Qh4 5. Nc3 Nf6 6. Nf5 Qh5 7. Be2 Qg6 8. Nh4 (Scotch Game).

CENTER COUNTER DEFENSE 214

Trapping

1. e4	d5
2. exd5	Qxd5
3. Nc3	Qa5
4. d4	Nf6
5. Nf3	Bg4
6. h3	Qh5
7. hxg4!	Qxh1
8. Ne2	Nxg4?

WHITE TO MOVE

Solution: Black's queen is trapped by **9. Ng3!**.

Comment: Black misses the threat to the queen. But it's unproductive to move the queen four times in the first eight moves anyhow. Try to rely more on the lighter forces. Three minor pieces can be an awesome force.

Related Zap: 1. e4 e5 2. Nf3 f6 3. Nxe5 fxe5 4. Qh5+ g6 5. Qxe5+ Qe7 6. Qxh8 Nf6 7. d3 d5 8. Bg5 Nbd7 9. Bxf6 Nxf6 10. f3 Kf7 11. Nd2 Bg7 (Damiano Defense).

Related Zap: 1. d4 Nf6 2. c4 d6 3. Nf3 Bg4 4. Nbd2 Nc6 5. d5 Nb8 6. Qb3 Nfd7 7. Qxb7 Nb6 8. c5 Bc8 (Queen Pawn Game).

Double Threat

1.	e4	d5
2.	exd5	Qxd5
3.	Nc3	Qa5
4.	d4	Nf6
5.	Nf3	Nc6
6.	d5	Nb4
7.	Bd2	Bd7
8.	Ne5	Nbxd5
9.	Bc4	Qc5?

WHITE TO MOVE

Solution: White wins a piece with **10. Bxd5 Nxd5 11. Nxd7 Kxd7 12. Be3.** After Black saves the queen, White takes the knight.

Comment: Black falls behind in development, which is exacerbated by the inability to develop the king bishop. White, on the other hand, has fluidity of movement, with both center pawns advanced and all minor pieces developed. That's a winning advantage.

Related Zap: 1. e4 c5 2. c3 d5 3. exd5 Qxd5 4. d4 cxd4 5. cxd4 Nc6 6. Nf3 Nf6 7. Nc3 Qa5 8. d5 Nb4 9. a3 Nbxd5 10. Bb5+ Bd7 11. Bxd7+ Kxd7 12. b4 (Sicilian Defense).

CENTER COUNTER DEFENSE **216**

Discovery

1. e4	d5
2. exd5	Qxd5
3. Nc3	Qa5
4. d4	Nf6
5. Nf3	Nc6
6. d5	Nb4
7. Bd2	Nbxd5
8. Bb5 +	c6

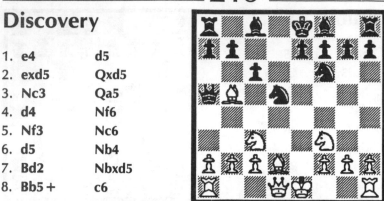

WHITE TO MOVE

Solution: White wins a piece with the discovery **9. Nxd5.** If 9. . . . Qxb5, then 10. Nc7+ wins the queen.

Comment: Black goes pawn-grabbing and drops a piece. But it isn't necessary to lose the queen. Instead of taking on b5, Black can withdraw the queen to d8. But then White exchanges knights on f6 (with check) and retreats the bishop to safety, staying a piece ahead.

Related Zap: 1. e4 e5 2. d4 exd4 3. Qxd4 Nc6 4. f4 Nf6 5. e5 d5 6. Qb5 a6 7. Qa4 b5 8. Qb3 Nd4 9. Qc3 Bb4 10. Qxb4 Nxd2 + (Center Game).

Mating Net

1. e4	d5
2. exd5	Qxd5
3. Nc3	Qa5
4. d4	Nf6
5. Nf3	Nc6
6. d5	Nb4
7. Bd2	Nbxd5
8. Bb5 +!	Kd8
9. Ne5	Nxc3?

WHITE TO PLAY

Solution: Knight takes on f7 for mate: **10. Nxf7 + +**.

Comment: Instead of answering White's ninth-move threat, Black proceeds to capture a knight and threaten White's queen. If you don't respond to your opponent's attacks, your opponent won't have to respond to yours.

Related Zap: 1. e4 c5 2. Nf3 d6 3. Ng5 Qc7 4. Bb5 + Kd8 5. Nxf7 + + (Sicilian Defense).

Glossary of Tactics

DESPERADO: A threatened or trapped piece sacrificed for the most it can get or to inflict damage.

DIRECT ATTACK: Moving a unit into position to capture another with advantage.

DISCOVERY: An attack by a stationary piece unveiled when a friendly unit moves out of its way.

DOUBLE THREAT: Two separate threats, not necessarily made by the same unit.

FORK: An attack by one unit against two different enemy units at the same time.

INTERFERENCE: Cutting the power of an enemy unit by putting a unit in the way, often with a time-gaining counterattack.

JETTISON: Forcing your opponent to sacrifice material to save the king or avoid loss of even greater material.

MATING ATTACK: A general onslaught against the king, resulting in mate or material gain.

MATING NET: A forced mate.

OVERLOAD: A situation in which a unit cannot fulfill all its defensive commitments.

PIN: An attack on an enemy unit that shields a more valuable unit.

REMOVING THE GUARD: Capturing or driving away a unit that guards another.

SAVING: Avoiding the loss of material, usually with a time-gaining threat.

SKEWER: An attack on an important unit that by moving exposes another unit to capture.

TRAPPING: Winning a unit that has no escape, usually by attacking it with less valuable units.

UNPIN: A counterattack that breaks a pin, gains time to break a pin, or ends a pin by eliminating or diverting a pinning unit.

Appendix 1:
Tactics Index
(Numbers refer to traps, not pages)

Appendix 2:
Related Zaps: Opening Index
(Numbers refer to traps, not pages)

Index

About the Author

Bruce Pandolfini is the author of fourteen instructional chess books, including *Pandolfini's Chess Complete; Chessercizes; More Chessercizes; Checkmate; Bobby Fischer's Outrageous Chess Moves; Principles of the New Chess; Pandolfini's Endgame Course; Russian Chess; The ABC's of Chess; Let's Play Chess; Kasparov's Winning Chess Tactics; One-Move Chess by the Champions; Chess Openings: Traps and Zaps; Square One;* and *Weapons of Chess.* He is also the editor of the distinguished two-volume anthology *The Best of Chess Life & Review,* and has produced, with David MacEnulty, two instructional videotapes, *Understanding Chess* and *Opening Principles.*

Bruce was the chief commentator for the New York half of the 1990 Kasparov-Karpov World Chess Championship. In the same year he was head coach of the United States Team in the World Youth Chess Championships in Wisconsin. Perhaps the most experienced chess teacher in North America, he is cofounder, with Faneuil Adams, of the Manhattan Chess Club School, and is the director of the New York City Schools Program. Bruce's most famous student, six-time National Scholastic Champion Joshua Waitzkin, is the subject of Fred Waitzkin's acclaimed book *Searching for Bobby Fischer.* Bruce Pandolfini lives in Manhattan.